LIGHTNING
EAST TO WEST

LIGHTNING EAST TO WEST

Jesus, Gandhi, and the Nuclear Age

JAMES W. DOUGLASS

Foreword by Archbishop Raymond Hunthausen

CROSSROAD · NEW YORK

TO MOTHER AND DAD, WHO KEPT GIVING LIFE

TO BOB AND JANET, WHO BELIEVED AND ACTED

TO DAVID, WHOSE VISIONS HELPED ME TO SEE

AND TO JIM, WHOSE ENDURING FAITH IS THE CHRIST IN ALOHA

1986

The Crossroad Publishing Company
370 Lexington Avenue
New York, New York 10017

Copyright © 1983 by James W. Douglass.

Printed in the United States of America

Library of Congress Cataloging in Publication Data

Douglass, James W.
Lightning East to West.

1. Atomic warfare—Religious aspects.
2. Nonviolence—Religious aspects.   I. Title.
BL65.A85D68   1983   261.8'73   83-7338
ISBN 0-8245-0587-5

Grateful acknowledgment is made to the following for permission to reprint material:

"What Did Jesus Discover?" first appeared in abbreviated form under the title "Non-violence and Metanoia" in the Winter 1974 issue of *Katallagete, Journal of the Committee of Southern Churchmen* (Vol. 5, No. 2) and in its entirety in *Gandhi Marg.*

"Lightning East to West" first appeared in *Gandhi Marg.*

"Invitation" under the title of "Living at the End of the World" appeared in slightly different form in *Fellowship.*

Other chapters were published earlier in *The Catholic Agitator.*

The quotation from Thomas Merton's unpublished work, *The Inner Experience,* is cited by permission of the Merton Legacy Trust.

Contents

We are not capable of union
with one another on the deepest level
until the inner self in each one of us
is sufficiently awakened to confront
the inmost spirit of the other.

Thomas Merton,
The Inner Experience

Foreword

This book illustrates once more that the most profound reflections upon the meaning of life can spring only from the thoughts of those who are deeply committed to that life. Out of his own journey—his association with British Columbia where he grew up, his marriage, his involvement with the peace movement, his contemplative immersion in the thought and spirit of Merton, Einstein, Jung, Gandhi, and ultimately Jesus himself—Jim Douglass has fashioned a nonviolent approach to the terrifying crisis situation of our time.

This work reveals that the author has grasped a progressively more unified vision. The one God operates in all persons and material creation to draw all being into unity. Hence there are common patterns to the thought of physicists, psychologists, and spiritual writers; hence one can find parallel experiences in the lives of diverse persons. In this perspective metanoia becomes the process by which one renounces one's isolated individuality and becomes attuned to the God who works in and through all to bring all into unity; and nonviolence becomes but the necessary means of acknowledging our oneness with all others.

I am in profound sympathy with this vision and its roots in Jesus' proclamation of the kingdom of God. I commend this book to all who are concerned with the promotion of peace in our time.

ARCHBISHOP RAYMOND HUNTHAUSEN

Preface

When work began on this book ten years ago, I understood its writing as a form of prayer. Jesus and Gandhi discovered a nonviolent process that offers inconceivable possibilities of change in our nuclear age. We need not despair. Hope is grounded in our very being, in a loving, truthful process bound up with it.

I have struggled to describe that process here, a process which is neither personal nor political but something fusing and transforming both—the kingdom of God, satyagraha. I believe it is a way open to each of us to transform the age of holocaust into a new beginning.

In the Gospel according to Matthew, Jesus describes the end of the world and the coming of the kingdom of God as "lightning striking in the east and flashing far into the west." (Matthew 24:27) We fear (and place our trust in) a different kind of lightning across the horizon today. We will choose lightning east to west today as either nuclear fire or the kingdom of God, as either despair and annihilation or transformation through nonviolence.

If we look to Jesus and Gandhi, and what they point to, we can hope to choose the lightning fire of nonviolence.

Acknowledgments

It is a deep gift to have as editor and publisher Johnny Baranski, whose own life touches everything I've tried to write about. Thank you, Johnny.

When you love many people, it's hard to choose a few for a dedication. Mother and Dad, Bob and Janet Aldridge, David Kerkkonen, and Jim Albertini have all had something special to do with this book. But I think of others, too, especially in the communities Shelley and I have lived and worked with: Catholic Action of Hawaii, Shanti, Pacific Life Community, and Ground Zero—incredible people in each. I think of them with love.

While working on this book in Hedley, British Columbia, I was helped at a critical time by W.H. and Carol Bernstein Ferry. I'm deeply grateful to them.

When I asked David Kerkkonen if he would consider doing a cover graphic, he looked first through his book of British Columbia pictographs and wrote:

"have found what i take to be maybe a lightning spirit   am working on a more anthropomorphic version—trying to get something at once reminiscent of primitive and western conceptions of lightning in its two aspects—illumination and holocaust

"the A-Bomb as a visionary experience?   the ultimate lightning   capable like lightning of transformation on two levels, though the spiritual side would depend on its *not* being exploded a transformation from the inside   i think *Lightning East to West* is primarily 'about' the transformation of the 'inner' man and woman, a coming to an understanding of the 'wilderness' "

David's understanding of that lightning, and his love, helped sustain the writing of this book. I'm grateful that his beautiful graphic is on the cover.

I wish Shelley's beauty could emerge as clearly from these pages as it has in my life. When Johnny asked me about someone to write an introduction, there was only one person. Our life together is where the book begins, suffers its way through, and ends.

Introduction

I've read this book several times as it was being written, and again later as a unit. Each time I've read it, it has prompted different thoughts. It's a book that hints at things just beyond the range of sight. It's exciting and inspiring to read it because each reading brings out different facets of what may be possible, and what may be required of us if the possible is to happen.

The movement for social change is rich in visions. We all seem to have our ideas of the perfect world, some including detailed economic and political systems, some simply a glorious dream of peace and love and harmony. We need both, of course. We need practical ideas of organization, and we need splendid ideas of harmony to inspire us. Sometimes, though, the visions of harmony seem so far removed from our lives as to be impossible, and disagreements on practical plans split us apart. Some day, "after the revolution," visions will be attainable. But now they are far away on the other side of that future event, change.

I think we need some sense of the connection that exists between the struggles and fragility of our own day-to-day unromantic lives and the ultimate goal, the vision. It's a platitude in the nonviolent movement to say that ends and means are determined by each other. Perhaps we don't really understand what that means. Because we tend to see our visions as being out there in the future, we don't connect our present lives with the dream that inspires them. I think Jim's book is important because it does that. It takes the mundane, painful, and downright unpleasant struggles we've been through and says here, this is where the vision lives; these are steps on the way to our dream. The steps were some of the hardest passages in our fourteen-year marriage; the fact that so far we've survived together is perhaps due to equal parts of mulishness and grace.

One thing I've learned from Jim is the importance of patience and persistence in relationship, the need to work through problems over long periods of time in an atmosphere of commitment. A marriage, a friendship, a love relationship, a social bond, a political coalition: All forms of relationship in process with many problems continually arising. The problems are bridges over time toward the vision of the future. The struggle is to see that, to stay with it, and to bring the faraway vision home to the present where it hurts most. Jim has often been able to do that for me with patience, persistence, and forgiveness. I hope this book can share some of our experiences with bridges.

The urgent sense of no-time in this book is also present in our lives, a counterbalance to the need for long term evolution: The sense that we may not *have* a long time. We may have months or years rather than decades or centuries. That sense of urgency was first shared with us by our friend Bob Aldridge, designer of the Trident missile. Bob told us of his discouragement at the widespread ignorance of nuclear issues: Machinery for a disarming nuclear first strike, he said, will be in place in less than ten years. When such a strike becomes possible for us but not yet for the other side, it's most likely to happen. And when it happens, it's too late to protest. You can't sit in front of a missile as it's being fired. The only time left to prevent nuclear war is the present. After talking to Bob we moved from Canada to live near the Trident base, to work more intensively in the anti-Trident movement. The urgency grows as we watch the submarine base grow. We continue to discuss, to leaflet, to march, to be arrested. People are listening and thinking. Change is occurring, but will it be in time? We feel a simultaneous need to live as if we had all the time in the world to love each other and foster lasting change, and again to live as though the world will end tomorrow if we aren't changed today.

When Jim and I first came together, we did so out of faith in a vision of the unity possible between us, and in that unity as a sign of human unity. We recognized the vision and the love between us as a gift. It was the kind of gift that can be received only by being risked. We didn't understand that at first. We do a bit better now. In the course of growing—together and separately—we've had to risk the love between us by challenging each other's actions and beliefs, by living long periods apart, by risking injury and sometimes death in nonviolent action. Any one of those risks could have ended our marriage. The risk was the offering back of the gift. So far the sense of unity has always been given back to us enriched and deepened. We think it would have faded and disappeared had we tried instead to protect it.

The risking of the gift of love gave us a hint as to the solution of the problem of time. Time is relative. We need to live our lives in relationship as if we have all the time (hence all the patience) in the world. We need to live our lives as though, without change, the world will end tomorrow. We need to offer the gift back to the giver. The solution is this: The offering back of the gift, risking whatever is most precious to us, telescopes time and assures us of the time we need truly to love the gift. Love becomes deeper in a shorter span of time because it is risked. Love, deepening in a short span of time, can change us in ways we don't see or know. Were we able to love deeply enough in a short enough time, we would be transformed. In being transformed, we could transform the world, and then we would have forever in which to love.

I think Jim's book is a direct challenge to bridge time with our lives; to offer back the most precious gifts, to telescope time and receive eternity.

Shelley Mae Douglass

1
What Did Jesus Discover?

We are told that Jesus once asked the people about John the Baptist, "What did you go out into the wilderness to see?" (Matthew 11:7) The question is an even more interesting one, though, when we turn it back on Jesus, because Jesus like John was a man of the wilderness. The question, when turned back on Jesus, is: "What did you, Jesus, go out into the wilderness to see?"

The question put another way is: What truth of reality did Jesus seek out and discover in his life and death? A second question, very close to the first, is: *How* did Jesus discover a particular truth of reality through his life and death? Jesus believed that the way is itself the truth. The question, *"What* did Jesus go out into the wilderness to see?"*, is also the question of the way of the wilderness. What way did Jesus follow in the wilderness, in the depths of himself, in order to discover a new reality? What is our way into that same reality?

Gandhi is helpful here in our understanding of the question. His secretary Pyarelal has described Gandhi's discovery of reality in relation to Einstein's:

> Einstein has given us his well-known equation setting forth the relationship between mass and energy which states that when even an infinitesimal particle of matter attains the velocity of light, the maximum velocity attainable in the physical world, it acquires a mass which is infinite. The corresponding law governing the release of spiritual energy is to be found in the formula enunciated by Gandhiji, viz. that even an infinitesimal of an individual, when he has realized the ideal of Ahimsa in its fullness so that in thought, word and deed, he—in short his whole being—becomes a function of Ahimsa as it were, he becomes filled with its power, the power of love, soul force, truth force, or the godhead within us, to which there is no limit and before which all opposition and hatred must cease: "With Satya combined with Ahimsa you can bring the whole world to your feet."[1]

According to Gandhi, the laws that govern the power of

nonviolent truth, or satyagraha, are as objective and concrete as physical laws. Gandhi discovered those laws through his experiments in truth.

I believe that Jesus also experimented in truth, and that what we are given in the Gospels about Jesus is the result of his experiments as transmitted through several layers of tradition. But it is the way of truth itself, what Jesus experimented in—what he did and what he came to see—which we have to discover if we want Jesus' reality to help us into our own new reality.

At a point in my life twenty years ago, a certain interior force combined with the example of friends urged me to experiment in the truth of the Sermon on the Mount. The example before me was that of a married couple with a growing family. Neither husband nor wife was employed. His vocation was that of a writer. This couple believed that God would care for them and their children if they sought out and did His daily will. They lived accordingly, totally reliant on Providence, and I witnessed the fact that what they believed about Providence came to pass.

Following my friends' example, I began to experiment in the same truth of the Sermon on the Mount, summed up by Jesus when he said: "So do not worry; do not say, 'What are we to eat? What are we to drink? How are we to be clothed?' It is the pagans who set their hearts on all these things. Your heavenly Father knows you need them all. Set your hearts on his kingdom first, and on his righteousness, and all these other things will be given you as well." (Matthew 6:31-33)

Virtually everything I had absorbed from my home and culture contradicted Jesus' teaching on this point, especially as it related to the care and security of my family. But constant experiments in following the will and way of the Reality Jesus called "the Father," at whatever apparent risk to self and family, have convinced me over the years that what Jesus taught in Matthew 6:33 describes a culturally hidden law of reality itself. I believe there is a loving, caring will at the center of reality which is as objective and concrete as a physical law. To experiment in its truth is to discover and confirm its reality.

The most deceptive characteristic of the Jesus of the Gospels is the ease with which he is described as stating a revolutionary principle like, "Set your hearts on his kingdom first, and on his righteousness, and all these other things will be given you as well." The Reality rooted in the world which that statement points to could never have been discovered by Jesus—could never have been envisioned, tested, and confirmed as true by the man Jesus—without his experiencing in the process the deepest suffering, doubt, and darkness, as the Gospels do in fact show at Gethsemane and on the cross. But the Gospels tell us nothing about how Jesus first discovered the way of absolute trust in the Reality behind Matthew 6:33. They give us only the principle of Jesus' reality as stated parabolically in the Sermon on the Mount. They do not describe the process whereby Jesus discovered it. They do not tell us his personal way into that reality. "What did you go out into the wilderness to see?"

I believe that many experiments in the truth of reality must have taken place during the 20-30 silent years of Jesus, before he began his public life by proclaiming the way of the kingdom with the authority described in the four Gospels. A Christian living today has little hope of attaining historical knowledge of those years of Jesus' life passed over by the Gospels, when Jesus struggled toward and arrived at the truths which the Gospels state with such certitude. But the Christian today has her or his own discoveries of the kingdom to make. And those discoveries, Jesus tells us, will come not by crying, Lord, Lord, but by ourselves doing the will of God—a will which we do know from the Gospels' account led Jesus into a final darkness and death. We can suppose that the culmination on the cross of all Jesus' experiments in truth was anticipated by each of the ego-deaths which resulted in his discoveries of the liberating truths of the Gospels. Behind each of those truths of the Gospel which introduces us into a new reality lies an ego-crucifixion of the person Jesus who first passed into that reality. The same baptism by fire is required of us to discover the kingdom's reality today.

For us to ask the question, then, "What did Jesus discover?" is to ask, "What can *we* discover through experiments in the reality described in the Gospel?"

In considering the question of experiments in a spiritual reality, first by Jesus and today by ourselves, it is helpful to follow Pyarelal's suggestion by reflecting on Albert Einstein's breakthrough theories and experiments in a physical reality. We can remember, first of all, that it is against the background of Einstein's work in physics that the question of spiritual change has been brought to a unique and terminal crisis in history.

We live in an end-time, i.e., a time in which the political and technological structures of the world make it probable that the human race will soon cease to exist. This end-time is, only in a physical sense, a partial result of Einstein's speculations. By deduction from his principle of relativity of mass, Einstein arrived at a conclusion whose pragmatic realization introduced us into the end of time. Einstein had seen that the mass of a body is not constant but varies with its state of motion. This principle of relativity of mass had been hidden from classical physics because the increase of mass in motion is infinitesimal until it attains a velocity relatively close to the speed of light. Einstein reasoned, from the relativity of mass, that energy itself has mass, and that therefore it must be possible to change one into the other. His equation concerning this mass-energy relationship (in which $c =$ the speed of light), $E = mc^2$, shows the almost inconceivable amount of concentrated energy contained in any particle of matter. The conversion of matter into such enormous energy, which first occurred in the New Mexico desert on July 16, 1945, is dependent on mass reaching a velocity close to the constant which Einstein found in the universe, the speed of light.

This discovery about the physical universe is worth reflecting on not only because it brought us into an end-time but because it was based on an intuition of Einstein's which may be helpful to our spiritual situation. Einstein believed in a universe whose laws are harmonious. Whenever Einstein was confronted by apparent conflicts or disharmonies in the classical physics, he refused to accept them, however obvious the conclusions seemed to be. We have to remember that Einstein's breakthrough came from his hypothesis of the critical importance of the speed of light as a universal constant, particularly in changing matter into energy. His critical factor for an inconceivable kind of change was itself beyond human senses and laboratory instruments, and beyond the imagination of his fellow scientists.

Is there a spiritual reality, inconceivable to us today, which corresponds in history to the physical reality which Einstein discovered and which led to the atomic bomb? Einstein discovered a law of physical change: the way to convert a single particle of matter into enormous physical energy. Might there not also be, as Gandhi suggested, an equally incredible and undiscovered law of spiritual change, whereby a single person or small community of persons could be converted into an enormous spiritual energy capable of transforming a society and a world?

I believe that there is, that there must be, a spiritual reality corresponding to $E = mc^2$ because, from the standpoint of creative harmony, the universe is incomplete without it, and because, from the standpoint of moral freedom, humankind is sentenced to extinction without it. I believe that the human imperative of our end-time is that we discover the spiritual equation corresponding to Einstein's physical equation, and that we then begin to experiment seriously in its world-transforming reality while there is time.

Jesus, we should recall, also lived in an end-time, or at least spoke and acted as if he did.

> With Jesus, the arrival of the last days, "eschatology," becomes the central symbolism for a radical intensification of moral concern. . . The effect of Jesus' symbolism is to place before us the destruction of the whole environment, natural and social, not as an hypothesis, but as a possible deserved event; and then have us reconsider who and what we are. Eschatology is necessary to his ethics. [2]

Biblical scholars have debated whether or not Jesus expected that the world would literally end in his generation, and many have followed Albert Schweitzer's thesis that Jesus did expect that the end would come soon. In any event, Jesus was living and speaking in a milieu of apocalyptic thought-forms in which the myth of the end of the world was common. John Pairman Brown says that the force of the myth "rests on the fact that it points to something real coming. The myth of the end of the world points to the fact of the end of the world,"[3] if not in Jesus' time, nevertheless true in some future time to his perception of the inexorable logic of human sin and its ever-widening destruction of the world:

> The New Testament myth of the end of the world is a true fore-shadowing of demonic technology; it sees the destruction of the physical environment as a direct consequence of social violence. . . .Jesus validates ethics by eschatology; ours is the first generation where the truth of his words has emerged from faith into history. [4]

Jesus' anticipation of a literal end may also in fact be a source of transformation regarding that end. Our assumption here is that Jesus in response to the crisis he perceived was an experimenter in that spiritual reality corresponding to Einstein's physical equation. The Gospels give us reasons for believing that Jesus discovered such a reality at extraordinary depths, and that the richness of those depths may be able to transform an otherwise end-time into a new beginning for the world. [5] We come back to Jesus, then, as both the proclaimer of an end-time and the personal way into a new world.

The causes of the world's imminent end in our time are humanly and technologically heightened forms of violence. A commitment to nonviolence would therefore seem to be basic today to the Gospels' personal way into a new world, and that has been my belief. But I have learned in my own experience just how distant a commitment to nonviolence can be from the transforming way of Jesus in the Gospels, how distant one's nonviolence may be in fact from the spiritual reality found in the wilderness—a spiritual reality which would be a true way of transformation in our end-time.

The end of the world, nonviolence, and the Catholic Worker were all introduced to me one morning in the spring of 1957 in a freshman English class at the University of Santa Clara. Herb Burke, our professor, passed out an article about a group of people in New York City who had refused to take shelter during a compulsory civil defense drill. Instead of going underground, these people, 29 of them as I recall, went into Central Park where they awaited arrest for being in the open. They said that to go into a shelter, assuming a hydrogen bomb was about to explode overhead, was not only futile but immoral: It was to say yes to the sin and crime of preparing for nuclear war. Better to go to jail, and they did.

With the other members of the class, I argued furiously against the witness of the people in the park and Herb Burke's persistent suggestion that they were right in their disobedience to the state. A friend in the class was disturbed to the point of later consulting a priest on the matter, who relieved his conscience by saying that Pope Pius XII had ruled out conscientious objection as a moral option for Catholics. I saw no priest but continued to brood over the people in the park and in jail, whom I now identified as Dorothy Day and the Catholic Worker community though there were others with them. By walking into Central Park that day, on their way to jail, the Catholic Worker community had generated a nonviolent force of truth whose waves eventually hit Governor Rockefeller's office (the civil defense drills were stopped as the numbers in the park multiplied) as well as more remote points like our classroom in California. For myself the most immediate effect, once my arguing subsided, was a sudden, burning awareness of a two-sided reality: That humanity in the

nuclear age was living at the end of time, and that a life based on
conscience was a real possibility.

That first encounter with Dorothy Day and the Catholic Worker
put me in living contact with a tradition whose richness has deepened
for me over the years—the tradition of faith and suffering love, at the
center of the Church and extending through centuries of martyrs
("witnesses") to the cross of Christ. As I began reading *The Catholic
Worker*, I recognized a community living out the Gospel, whose
professions of nonviolence represented the life of Christ in the
America of the 50's: a life of voluntary poverty in service to the
involuntarily destitute, a life of following Providence, of practicing
the works of mercy, of resisting a warfare state with nonviolent civil
disobedience; a life and way corresponding to Jesus' cross. My
introduction to nonviolence, through the Catholic Worker, was
therefore an experience embodied in a community of faith, within the
global context of an impending nuclear end of time.

It was also in the pages of *The Catholic Worker*, four years later
in 1961, that I saw Thomas Merton's first published words on the
moral issue which had taken hold of my own life and writing, the
issue of nuclear war. Merton had written a stark poem, "Chant to Be
Used in Processions around a Site with Furnaces," a string of
apocalyptic images recalled with satisfaction by the commander of a
Nazi death-camp—a detailing of the system's clean efficiency for
Jews and the Nazis' perfect obedience to it, then the final stanza:

> Do not think yourself better because you burn up
> friends and enemies with long-range missiles without
> ever seeing what you have done. [6]

Dorothy Day and the Catholic Worker had introduced me to
nonviolence in a community of faith. Tom Merton, in his intense
essays on war, peace, and nonviolence which followed the
appearance of his "Chant," showed the contemplative dimension of
nonviolence, that dimension of inner unity which made deep sense of
the fact that a Hindu, Gandhi, could be the greatest modern example
of the way of Christ, the way of suffering love to the point of death
and transformation. Nonviolence in deed, said Merton, was nothing
more than a living out of a nonviolence of the heart, an inner unity
already experienced in prayer, as Gandhi had emphasized in
rejecting the more popular concept of nonviolence as a political tactic.
Gandhi's nonviolent doctrine of satyagraha, or truth-force, like the

nonviolent cross of Jesus, was based not on effectiveness but on
faith—involving a renunciation of the fruits of action in simple
obedience to God's will, a loving, unifying will which in a world of
injustice took one inevitably to one's cross.

Tom Merton's contemplative life and writings gradually revealed
to me the most radical dimension of nonviolence, that inner unity in
silent prayer without which nonviolent tactics were liable to descend
from truth-force to "duragraha" (a biased, manipulative strategy), as
happened increasingly in the civil rights, peace, and campus
demonstrations of the 60's, from there to drain away finally in
sporadic violence and mass apathy.

A few days before he was assassinated, Gandhi said to a friend:
"Have nothing to do with power."[7] Merton's life was a paradigm of
that politically scandalous tenet of nonviolence, a continuous
following of a spiritual instinct which withdrew him from even the
most subtle forms of spiritual power—so that in 1968 at a critical
point in resistance to the war, which Merton himself suffered
intensely within, his final pilgrimage was not to a courtroom or a jail,
as I and others wished then, but to points beyond Vietnam in search
of an inner fire whose exact meaning for us remains unclear today.

In reflecting on what it meant for me, as a Catholic college
student of the late 50's-early 60's to learn nonviolence from Dorothy
Day and Thomas Merton, I feel the immense grace of the Gospel
tradition conveyed by their lives—and in Merton's case, the grace of
those other spiritual traditions from the East which he was absorbing
into a universal Christ. Because of their lives, I knew nonviolence less
as a strategy for social change than as a force of truth and love which
had become real in them, and could become real in others, from the
Reality at the Gospel's center.

But even given the profound gift of that Gospel perspective on
nonviolence, I found in my own life that each act of nonviolent
resistance to the war which I joined in during the late 60's raised for
whatever community I was in, and for me personally, the ever-more-
urgent question of impotence before and within an overwhelming
evil. We knew too little in our own lives of the powerless power of
Christ in Dorothy Day and Thomas Merton. In our acts of resistance,
we were brought back again and again to the need for a deeper base,
or for a rock outside the world on which to stand. The deeper question
in the fact of our government's violence was not one of becoming
more effective against it but of reaching that inner point out of which

one could respond more fully, more deeply, more unitedly, to the visible and invisible nature of evil. The suffering from the war continued to be so overwhelming that one clearly could and had to go deeper, infinitely deeper, in one's life toward an unrealized center of grace out of which an altogether new and transforming kind of nonviolence could then arise. The Gospels called such a possibility *metanoia*. Tom Merton's writings gave clues on what metanoia might mean for us. I sought it by withdrawing to my home in the British Columbia mountains for a year and writing the book *Resistance and Contemplation.*

I believe that nonviolence reconsidered after the experiences of the 60's can only mean the continuing search for that far deeper center of the inner dimension of nonviolence, which would be expressed less in action than in transformation, whose discovery is the spiritual (and political) imperative of our nuclear end-time, and toward which I believe Tom Merton was somehow pointing in his journey to the East.

It is an event which occurred in March 1972, however, after the writing of *Resistance and Contemplation*, which has underlined for me that lesson of the nonviolence of the 60's which I learned first from Dorothy Day and Tom Merton, the absolute need for metanoia at a depth which, for the sake of self-survival, we would rather not even glimpse or sense. The event which brought the lesson home was the pouring of blood on top-secret electronic warfare files in Pacific Air Force Headquarters, Hickam Air Base, Hawaii.

The Hickam action was one of the most miraculous events I have experienced in a life which I can honestly understand only as a series of miracles. I think the use of the term "miracle" here is accurate in the sense that the realities overridden providentially at Hickam would be regarded by almost all of us as being at least as binding on our freedom as are physical laws. Yet, in spite of that miraculous aspect of Hickam, the same event has in retrospect opened up a darkness in myself which is a deeper need for metanoia all over again. It is necessary to speak of the first aspect of Hickam to get to the second.

Our way of access to the top-secret files of Pacific Air Force Headquarters was through a series of opening gates, doors, and file drawers at the base: The first opening occurred one day when a friend and I, while driving to the base in preparation for a demonstration in front of it, got into the wrong lane of traffic and instead of being stopped were waved through the front gate by the security guard despite the fact that our car displayed no security sticker. Surprised and encouraged, we drove further to the Headquarters Building, and I tried to enter it from a side entrance. No one stopped me. In spite of the electronic eyes scanning the hallways and signs warning of the possibility of search at any time, I was on that occasion able to consult a wall directory and explore that area of the building briefly, again without being stopped.

A week later, on a second visit to the Headquarters Building, I was stopped in a hallway: by a sergeant who instead of asking for my credentials (for which I had made no preparation) asked if he could help me. I told him, yes, that I was looking for the Electronic Warfare Wing. He courteously escorted me to it, then went about his business, leaving me free to explore the corridors of that specific part of Pacific Air Force Headquarters responsible for the electronic battlefield in Indochina.

That was the extent of our inside knowledge, a knowledge of certain entrances and corridors, when seven of us went into the different wings of Pacific Air Force Headquarters on the afternoon of March 2, 1972. We had planned our action as a "leafletting invasion" of the Headquarters Building, one step in a continuing Lenten campaign of nonviolent resistance at Hickam. On the eve of our leafletting invasion, two of us, Jim Albertini and I, decided to carry blood as well as leaflets, on the almost inconceivable chance that top-secret papers might somehow become accessible to us in high security offices we had never set foot in.

On the following afternoon, I was escorted again through the building by an Air Force sergeant, this time bearing a sealed envelope I had given him (which contained our statement on the war) addressed to the specific office I wanted to enter, the Programs/Planning Division of the Directorate of Electronic Warfare. It was in that office that I was left alone, standing before the desk of a major who had been given the envelope by the sergeant and was taking it to his commanding officer. And it was there that I saw for the first time, behind the major's desk, a metal filing cabinet with the words "Top Secret" printed across the top. There was a large lock on the filing cabinet, but the lock was open and the second file drawer slightly ajar. I took the container of blood from my briefcase and poured it over that drawer of file folders, then opened the top drawer and continued pouring blood on it until I was thrown to the floor and choked for what seemed a long time by the major.

The successive opening up of Pacific Air Force Headquarters' gates, doors, and files, after a graceful Reality put us in the wrong (right) lane of traffic, was what made it possible for us to break through the public silence of Hawaii's militarism during the year of the most intense bombing of Indochina. In that year, in our Lenten campaign at Hickam and in our trial and noncooperation with the sentence, we explored and experienced what Gandhi termed "experiments in truth."

Yet it is the second aspect of the Hickam action, its personal darkness in the midst of grace, which brings me back to the lesson of the nonviolence of the 60's, the still deeper need for metanoia.

In the case of Shelley and me and our marriage, the question we faced concerning acts of nonviolent resistance to the war which risked long prison sentences was never, whether or not we should be involved in them, but rather the more specific question: In particular situations of risk, which of us should be involved? The source of that question was our responsibility for our children, and our feeling that in any specific arrest situation only one of us should take part, so that the other would remain free to be with the children. But we both felt deeply the suffering of the war and the need to act.

In the Lenten campaign at Hickam, we had agreed that she would take part in civil disobedience first, in an action bearing a relatively low-risk arrest penalty. We also agreed that if a way appeared in the campaign for a higher-risk action involving access to top-secret materials, I would take part in that action. But on the eve of the Hickam "leafletting invasion," Shelley was home with the children while the final planning session took place elsewhere. It was at that session that Jim and I decided to carry blood, to be used in the event we had access to top-secret materials. When I returned home from the meeting and told Shelley, she felt that I had violated our agreement that she would act first, and that my acting now would foreclose any action of hers. I thought our agreement had meant the higher-risk action could come when an opening appeared, which was remote at any time and should be prepared for the following day. We now recognize that the agreement was ambiguous enough for each of us to understand it differently, but then we saw only our own sides. After we had argued the point for hours, I resolved to go ahead with the decision I had made at the planning session, in spite of Shelley's thinking it wrong.

That resolution is what I have had to recognize as the deep violation of convictions and feelings in the person I love most. Because of it, Shelley has been forced since that day to live a dual existence regarding the Hickam action, believing deeply in the action itself and supporting me for it, while knowing herself that I went ahead and did it without our having resolved a deep conflict between us. She has lived lovingly and truthfully through that situation created by me but not acknowledged in my heart and mind until more than two years after the event. The fact that she has come out on the other side of that violation of her still somehow believing in our marriage and in nonviolence has shown me the Gospel's center again, as I once experienced it from Dorothy Day and Tom Merton.

Metanoia is not simply a "change of mind," as it translates literally from the Greek. In its Gospel sense it means a change of heart and soul, an imperative continually arising from Reality itself if we wish to choose the fullness of freedom. The possibility of that full freedom coming into being for me in the nonviolence at Hickam was lost by my hardness of heart toward Shelley the night before. But there were other forces at work in our community and at Hickam, and I believe it was because of them that a grace-filled way opened up to the files—because of the uncompromised nonviolence of the other six members of our invading group, particularly Jim Albertini, a brother who simply embodies the Gospel, and Rose Brennan, our sister who fasted quietly and to exhaustion the full 40 days of Lent while continuing to work full-time in our office and to keep vigil, leaflet, and demonstrate as much as anyone. Reality opens to such lives. Thus Hickam opened its gates and its files.

Nonviolence reconsidered means a recognition in metanoia that the darkness of faith has to be complete for the satyagrahi when she/he chooses life. That darkness is the way of self-renunciation and the cross taught by Jesus and Gandhi, the continuing way of the Catholic Worker. On the eve of the Hickam action, when both Shelley and I felt profound, and we thought conflicting, convictions about acting for life, the way of metanoia would have been begun by my opening to her concern regardless of its consequences to my own. And had there been such an opening—in looking back now—there was the further, unrecognized possibility of our deciding to act together the next day at Hickam, in the total darkness that would have meant for us and our children—the kind of decision we did in fact make together later, when we decided we would both non-cooperate in court with our judge at the risk of simultaneous imprisonment. In reflecting now on that as a possibility at Hickam as well, I believe that such an earlier joint decision in faith would have taken us at the beginning to an inner center where a transforming nonviolence could have simply taken over our lives in Hawaii.

Our concern for our children was genuine, and short of the Gospel: There *is* a Father who is Mother and who lives at the heart of faith's darkness, who cares and responds as Jesus said. That One is one with the human family, a big community. There are many in whom that One lives as the fullness of love, who care and would have cared for our children, had the darkness of faith taken us to that darkness of fact. In fact, it has not (in our noncooperation in court, the judge backed away from jailing us) but perhaps we are more open to that darkness now than we were at first. Metanoia, the Gospel reminds us, is an urgent but continuing possibility—and through it, the continuing possibility of a nonviolent Love to transform the world.

Tom Merton at the conclusion of one of his last works, *Mystics and Zen Masters*, cut through our nonviolent postures in the West and identified precisely the arrogant weakness of our hearts. He questioned there "the Western acceptance of a 'will to transform others' in terms of one's own prophetic insight accepted as a norm of pure justice." He suggested to nonviolent activists:

> Is there not an "optical illusion" in an eschatological spirit which, however much it may appeal to *agape*, seeks only to transform persons and social structures *from the outside*? Here we arrive at a basic principle, one might almost say an ontology of nonviolence, which requires further investigation. [8]

It was that further investigation into an ontology of nonviolence which Merton was engaged in when he died in Bangkok in 1968. But the inner, transforming power of his life had already been given to us.

Tom Merton, Dorothy Day, and Shelley Douglass, I thank you for your lives.

To return to Einstein's equation for an inconceivable physical change in the world, $E = mc^2$, we can recall that the key factor in the equation was the speed of light, the constant in Einstein's universe. Only when the velocity of a particle of matter approached the speed of light could it be converted into a previously unimaginable physical energy.

I believe that if we were to formulate an analogous equation for an inconceivable spiritual change in the world, the key factor in the equation would be the power of Reality when engaged lovingly, truthfully, and at a depth of metanoia normally inconceivable to us, as it was inconceivable to me in my blindness toward Shelley.

The power of Reality to transform and unite us spiritually is seldom experienced even remotely because we seldom engage it. Unless we begin to experiment with reality, in the faith that a new Reality does lie within, the opening to the new—the security guard waving us onto the base, escorting us to the files—does not occur. An attempt to engage Reality means risk and loss, a loss of the self we identify with securely and privately, the self which doesn't want to believe in any reality beyond itself.

An experiment in reality is ultimately public. Such an experiment begins privately and personally, in the depths of prayer, consciousness, and the self—the first steps of metanoia and Jesus' reason for going out into the wilderness—*to see*, to see the possibility of a new Reality, perhaps inconceivable from his consciousness in Nazareth. But the new contemplative vision once realized requires practice and proclamation. The personal experiment in truth has to engage Reality ultimately in the community, and in the public order. Jesus didn't die on a private cross. Jesus' public life, the cleansing of the temple in which he forced the issue, and the consequent cross, brought him the ultimate metanoia, self-emptying, and engagement with Reality. In the same way, the rigorous experiments in eating and other personal habits described by Gandhi in his autobiography were completed in Gandhi's public experiments in voluntary suffering to free India from the British Empire.

The common factor in Jesus' and Gandhi's private and public experiments in reality is that all their experiments made them poor, increasingly poor in their very being. The voluntary poverty of the wilderness was completed by the state-enforced poverty of the cross. Jesus' and Gandhi's experiments in a public reality forced them into a still deeper poverty, realized in arrest, personal humiliation, and execution or assassination. An engagement with Reality at this depth is the spiritual constant analogous to the speed of light, which few approach closely enough to begin to initiate the spiritual change analogous to the physical transformation of the atom. The spiritual constant is self-emptying love for the sake of others, at an inconceivable depth in ourselves. The deeper the love, the more it will necessarily merge one's life with the life of all humanity, and thus approach the spiritual constant. In that perspective the crucifixion of Jesus is the absolute opening and invitation into a new Reality.

We therefore have to point our lives ultimately toward the public order in our experiments in reality, but in such a way that in moving into that order the vision of the wilderness remains intact. To keep that vision intact Gandhi like Jesus laid great emphasis on a day-to-day, self-emptying service of one's brothers and sisters in very concrete, personal ways. He called it "the constructive program." The constructive program is a sustained way of metanoia for the ultimate opening to the new Reality. In the course of its service one's life very naturally becomes more selfless, more communal, more at one with a widening world—what I have witnessed in such lives as Thomas Merton's, Dorothy Day's, and Shelley Douglass'. The living realization of one world, one Reality, is the goal, and a goal reached ultimately only through the spiritual constant of complete sacrifice. Just as the particle of matter has to be accelerated enough to attain the velocity necessary to split the atom, our day-to-day service of those around us has to accelerate our own community toward that point of complete sacrifice which is the spiritual speed of light.

An example and symbol of the problem is the Hickam action, in which a failure to recognize and serve the living Christ in Shelley meant a further failure to travel more deeply into the heart of faith's darkness—which could have struck a transforming light for others. We don't want to travel too deeply toward that transforming light whose only access is impenetrable darkness. None of us do. Yet the darkness of our end-time is already global.

What did Jesus go out into the wilderness to see? What did Jesus discover? The same spiritual constant as inconceivable as the speed of light which we must re-discover if our end-time, like his, is to be transformed by a light that shines in the dark, a light that darkness could not overpower.

1 Pyarelal, *Mahatma Gandhi: The Last Phase* (*Vol. II*) (Navajivan Publishing House: 1958), p. 789.

2 John Pairman Brown, *The Liberated Zone* (John Knox Press: 1969), p. 108.

3 *ibid.,* p. 109.

4 *ibid., pp. 111-12.*

5 Joachim Jeremias in his *New Testament Theology* concedes that "Jesus' expectation of an imminent end was one that remained unfulfilled. . .Jesus expected that the end would come soon." Joachim Jeremias, *New Testament Theology* (Scribners: 1971), p. 139. But he goes on to qualify this by two further points:

> First, the sayings of Jesus in which there is a note of the expectation of an imminent end are not apocalyptic speculations, forecasts of a date—Jesus rejected that quite firmly—but spiritual judgments. Their basic theme is: the hour of fulfillment has dawned, the reign of God is already being manifested here and now; soon the catastrophe introducing its definitive coming will arrive. Make use of the time before it is too late; it is a matter of life or death. If we want to sum up these spiritual judgments in one sentence, we might say that God has granted a last period of grace. The most important function of eschatology is that it keeps alive knowledge of this respite.
>
> The second point is even more important. Jesus himself added an astounding qualification to the sayings which presuppose that the end is near: God can *shorten* the time of distress for the sake of the elect who cry to him day and night (Luke 18.7f.); he can hear the cry 'Thy kingdom come'. . .On the other hand, however, God can also hear the request, 'Let it alone this year also', and *lengthen* the period of grace (Luke 13.6-9). Thus Jesus takes into account the possibility that God may rescind his own holy will. These sayings are among the most powerful spoken by Jesus. . .Jesus sets God's grace above his holiness. It can shorten the time of distress for his people and lengthen the opportunity for the unbelievers to repent. All human existence, hourly threatened by the catastrophe, lives in the interval of grace: 'Let it alone this year also, in case it perhaps bears fruit' (Luke 13.8f.). Jeremias, pp. 139-40.

6 The poem appeared also in Merton's *Emblems of a Season of Fury* (New Directions: 1963), pp. 43-7.

7 Gandhi spoke these words to Vincent Sheean, who had made a pilgrimage to him from America convinced that Gandhi was soon to die. Vincent Sheean, *Lead. Kindly Light* (Random House: 1949), p. 186.

8 Thomas Merton, *Mystics and Zen Masters* (Dell: 1967), pp. 287-8.

2
Lightning East to West

In the Gospel according to Matthew, Jesus says in his discourse on the end of the world, "The coming of the Son of Man will be like lightning striking in the east and flashing far into the west." (Matthew 24:27)

The light of the Second Coming: A single blinding flash, spanning east to west, instantaneous.

Jesus' image of the end of the world is like nothing so much as a nuclear blast in the sky. Yet the positive meaning of Jesus' image of the end, the victory of Truth and Love in history, is the exact opposite of a nuclear holocaust, which would be the ultimate human blasphemy against creation's meaning.

Lightning east to west can be adopted as the image of our end-time. We live in that final time which offers humans the clearest choice in history: the kingdom or the holocaust. Either end is a lightning east to west: the nuclear holocaust a lightning fire, the kingdom of Reality a lightning spirit.

Nuclear weapons are our immediate means of ending history. The prospect of a history-ending war increases with each new weapon in the arms race. We are told now by conservative experts who once put their faith in nuclear deterrence that nuclear war is becoming a political certainty:

Sober assessors such as George Rathjens of MIT and Thomas Schelling of Harvard, some of whom dismissed such talk 15 years ago as irresponsible, now say that a nuclear war is "inevitable" by 1999. The Stockholm Institute for Peace Research, which carries on the most comprehensive and thorough analysis of the nuclear arms race, comes to similar conclusions. [1]

Former Trident missile-designer Robert Aldridge, who has made the most systematic study of nuclear counterforce or first-strike weapons, fears that unless major changes occur by the mid 80s, we will have reached the point of no return. Nuclear first-strike technology will then start going into place, or be so far developed that any further resistance to nuclear war may simply be too late.[2]

While the nuclear powers escalate weapons systems, desperate hunger and oppression grow in the world—an invitation to a blackmail use of nuclear weapons by insurgent groups, whose capacity to obtain nuclear material and assemble it into a bomb grows proportionately to the rapid spread in the world of nuclear power plants (all producers of bomb material as a side effect). The hijacking of plutonium traveling from such a plant (or its purchase through an underground nuclear market) for the making of a bomb to blackmail whole cities and countries has become an increasingly conscious possibility in the world of terrorism, one whose effects we may all feel soon. The desperate will have their day with the Bomb.

In the face of these political and nuclear realities, the only species-sustaining choice open to humanity in our end-time is a global partnership of peoples, a world community based on a revolutionary transformation of values which can be called here the kingdom of Reality: kingdom because of the biblical vision involved; Reality because realism and faith are one in an end-time.

The kingdom of Reality can be defined, in terms of both process and goal, as a nonviolent community of justice and love seeking its extension to a global community of the same nature, through deepening self-sacrifice. The symbols and prophets of the kingdom of Reality are Jesus and Gandhi: Jesus, the kingdom's proclaimer and symbol in the West (but himself a Jew from the Mid-East); Gandhi, the kingdom's symbol in the East (but himself a student of the West in his reading of Thoreau, Tolstoy, and Ruskin). Their kingdom of nonviolent truth-force and love-force if realized would be a lightning east to west, the energy equivalent and alternative to a nuclear fire ending the world.

It was Albert Einstein at the beginning of the century who pointed out the real possibility of a previously inconceivable physical energy, and thus in effect prophesied nuclear fire. More recently it has been C.G. Jung who indicated the further possibility of an equally powerful, even more inconceivable (because unconscious) spiritual energy. Einstein's hypothesis has been tried and proven. Jung's has not been tried.

By his Special Theory of Relativity, Einstein showed that matter and energy are two aspects of a convertible reality, and that the amount of energy contained in any particle of matter is almost inconceivable. His equation, $E = mc^2$, in which the potential energy of any piece of matter is equal to its mass multiplied by the square of the speed of light, reveals the tiniest parts of our world as virtually infinite energy.

Einstein introduced humankind to an inner side of matter whose energy was beyond experience and imagination. That insight has been put to work by the weapons technicians, so that today we are aware of what the inner side of matter can do to the world in which we live when its energy is released through instantaneous chain reactions. The energy within small chunks of matter is capable of destroying all life on earth.

C.G. Jung gained insight into the world of infinite energy not from the standpoint of matter, as did Einstein, but from the standpoint of the psyche. But Jung felt there was a profound harmony between all forms of existence, and toward the end of his life he suggested the possibility of an ultimate agreement between psychic and physical forms of energy. He said at one point:

> Sooner or later nuclear physics and the psychology of the unconscious will draw closer together as both of them, independently of one another and from opposite directions, push forward into transcendental territory, the one with the concept of the atom, the other with that of the archetype.
>
> . . . Psyche cannot be totally different from matter, for how otherwise could it move matter? And matter cannot be alien to psyche, for how else could matter produce psyche? Psyche and matter exist in one and the same world, and each partakes of the other, otherwise any reciprocal action would be impossible. If research could only advance far enough, therefore, we should arrive at an ultimate agreement between physical and psychological concepts.[3]

The deep sense which Carl Jung had of an ultimate harmony between the psychic and the physical recalls that fundamental intuition by Einstein of a physical harmony in the universe, which impelled him beyond apparent inconsistencies to his greatest discoveries. Jung's sense of a psychic-physical harmony is necessary for any realistic hope of human survival. We can hope for humanity's future if we can believe that the inconceivable energy for physical change which Einstein pointed to has its parallel for spiritual change in the depths of the psyche. If this is not true, there is a profound disharmony between physical and spiritual forms of energy which will sentence humankind inevitably to extinction, through the constant historical factors of exploitation and war continued in the nuclear age.

The only realistic alternative to a doomsday vision inevitable from the history we know is the discovery of a power for human, global change as inconceivable to us today as the power of atomic energy was to humanity before Einstein. It is worth emphasizing here the need for such a discovery to be rooted in an experimental, verifiable way in the reality of the psyche or spirit, rather than in any of the salvation schemes of those seeking a way out of history. What the intuition of psychic-physical harmony would mean, if ever verified, is that there is a spiritual reality for change in humankind equal in energy to the physical reality of a nuclear explosion. The search for such a transforming reality is the overwhelming imperative of our end-time.

How can we discover such a kingdom of Reality through the deepest symbol we have of its power in the West, Jesus Christ?

Jung said of Christ's relation to the psyche:

> The Christ-symbol is of the greatest importance for psychology in so far as it is perhaps the most highly developed and differentiated symbol of the self, apart from the figure of the Buddha...The inclusion in a religion of a unique human personality—especially when conjoined to an indeterminable divine nature—is consistent with the absolute individuality of the self, which combines uniqueness with eternity and the individual with the universal. The self is a union of opposites *par excellence*, and this is where it differs essentially from the Christ-symbol. The androgyny of Christ is the utmost concession the Church has made to the problem of opposites. The opposition between light and good on the one hand and darkness and evil on the other is left in a state of open conflict, since Christ simply represents good, and his counterpart the devil, evil. This opposition is the real world problem, which at present is still unsolved. [4]

Christ, for Jung, was the Western symbol of the self because, like the self, Christ combined uniqueness with eternity and the individual with the universal. In one important respect, however, Jung felt that Christ differed from the psychological phenomenology of the self, in such a way that the Western mind has in Christ a profound—because of his conjoining of human and divine natures—yet incomplete symbol of the self. The critical difference with the self is that in Christ there is no reality of evil. What the Western psyche experiences, therefore, does not correspond to its archetype, Christ:

> In the empirical self, light and shadow form a paradoxical unity. In the Christian concept, on the other hand, the archetype is hopelessly split into two irreconcilable halves, leading ultimately to a metaphysical dualism—the final separation of the kingdom of heaven from the fiery world of the damned.[5]

The initial importance of this point can be brought home by comparing the man Jesus with the man Gandhi. (The comparison could also be made with Gautama, but Gandhi is more accessible to us in history.) For us the deep truth of Gandhi lies not in what Gandhi was but rather in what Gandhi became, because as Gandhi often insisted, any person at all could change in life just as much as he did: "I have not the shadow of a doubt that any man or woman can achieve what I have, if he or she would make the same effort and cultivate the same hope and faith."[6] Gandhi had to *become* Gandhi. A reading of Gandhi's *Experiments in Truth* reveals just how painful a process that becoming was. What we know in history as "Gandhi" and identify with the power of nonviolence emerged only after years of experiments in nonviolent truth. The would-be British gentleman studying law in London in 1888 named Mohandas Gandhi was not a likely prospect to lead a revolution against the British Empire. The revolutionary truth of Gandhi lies in what he became through his experiments, an objective force of truth and love, what Gandhi called "a satyagrahi".

If Gandhi's life is, as he claims, an example of the possible, then the most characteristic quality of Reality is its readiness to open up through experiments in truth. Reality invites each person into a step-by-step process characterized, in terms of the ego and its securities, by inexorable sacrifice and reducing one's self to zero. Experiments in the truth of Reality will follow the pattern of a constant disciplined probing of the outer walls of one's limitations, where the pure grace of Reality extends the truth beyond any individual's capacity to see the way forward and confers on that truth an objective power of change. The inconceivable becomes real. In this sense Jesus' view of Reality is the same as Gandhi's: "Ask, and it will be given to you; search, and you will find; knock, and the door will be opened to you.'' (Matthew 7:7) The way into an inconceivable Reality is through experiments in truth based on faith: "I tell you solemnly, if your faith were the size of a mustard seed you could say to this mountain, 'Move from here to there,' and it would move; nothing would be impossible for you.'' (Matthew 17:20-21)

The truth of Jesus, like the truth of Gandhi, lies in what he became. What Jesus became is also an objective force of truth and love, which in his case meets us through the Gospels of Matthew, Mark, Luke, and John, and in the community which lives out the truth of the Gospels. But therein also lies a critical difference, for the truth-force of the man Jesus as revealed in the four Gospels meets us exclusively in terms of what he finally became. The process of becoming has been lost to us: We know very little of Jesus before he began his public life, and virtually nothing of his inner growth. The four evangelists wrote no story of Jesus' experiments in truth. Their purpose was rather to proclaim the Good News of what Jesus had become, which was identical with what God had done with Jesus in raising him from death into a living, objective force of truth and love known as "the Christ".

But it can be suggested today that the growth in truth of Jesus the man is closer to our lives, and more dangerous to our securities (our failures to become), than is our confession of him as Christ, just as Gandhi the man as an experimenter in truth, as a living process of becoming, is a more redemptive reality than is the Mahatma, a conception which Gandhi himself rejected totally, just as many biblical scholars hold Jesus rejected the identification of himself as the Christ or Messiah.

This is what Jung was pointing toward as a more complete symbol of the self—a Jesus who *became* the objective force of truth and love proclaimed in the Gospels and whose actual life therefore spanned the opposites of existence during his experiments in truth in the same way each person's life must. Gandhi was not originally what he became. Nor was Jesus originally what he became. The truth of Jesus, like the truth of Gandhi, lies in what he became through the will and power of a deeper Reality, and lies therefore in what each person in the world can also become in grace. John's Gospel points in this direction in Jesus' statement, "I tell you most solemnly, whoever believes in me will perform the same works as I do myself, he will perform even greater works, because I am going to the Father.'' (John 14:12) By Jesus' going into a deeper Reality through his death, the objective power of the Spirit has been released. The way has been opened. Whoever believes in Jesus' way deeply enough, a way of life and death which is a way of seeking the further release of an objective love-force in history, will perform the same works as he did, and even greater works—which are absolutely necessary today for the continuation of human history.

What we have to deal with, then, if we view Jesus like Gandhi in this way, is a transformation hypothesis. The hypothesis can be stated as follows:

Every living person is capable, through a particular process, of creating the conditions for the expression of an objective love-force in history, a power of Reality beyond any of us which can raise humankind from the global death of our end-time.

This process of creating the conditions for transformation is characterized by Jesus' description, "He who loses his life will find it," and by Gandhi's axiom that the satyagrahi realizes the nature of truth-force only when s(he) has reduced herself to zero.

This process is characterized also by the driving of inner and outer worlds to a point of absolute oneness, an explosive oneness as is brought about by the energy polarities of the atomic bomb. Jesus and Gandhi created the conditions of spiritual-political explosions across the world through the deliberate giving of their lives while confronting evil, thus reducing themselves to zero as completely as would a person who set off an atomic bomb while standing next to it. But a satyagrahi is even closer to the reality of truth-force than is such a detonator, as it is her very life, like the matter in the atomic bomb, uranium or plutonium, which will be transformed into an explosive energy for changing others. Yet that energy is an objective force for change greater than the life or matter through which it happened to enter the world. The power of Christ upon history, which is an objective Reality of love-force, is far greater than that of Jesus of Nazareth, just as the objective reality of truth-force which Gandhi mediated by his life is greater than that life itself.

The transformation hypothesis will stand or fall on the assumption that there exists an objective Reality for change which is the spiritual equivalent of $E = mc^2$. That assumption can be proven only by experiments at the center of our lives. The key to proceeding in those experiments is to realize radically that it is not so much our lives which count but rather whatever reality for change can enter the world through them. Our lives are like the un-mined uranium destined for a particular atomic bomb: Scattered and hidden beneath the earth, the uranium's power for change is slight. When it has been mined, and progressively purified and integrated by a series of experiments, however, the uranium can be brought gradually to the point of a nuclear explosion, whereby it is re-scattered across the world with an inconceivable energy. Neither at the beginning nor at the end of this process is it the particular bits of uranium which are our concern but rather the power present beneath them. When that infinite power has been released, obliterating the uranium as we know it, the uranium's purpose in the experiments has been accomplished. So it is with our lives as we experiment in Reality.

A story from Shelley's and my life is helpful:

During the summer of 1972, the community with which Shelley and I worked, catholic Action of Hawaii, was preparing in Honolulu for the trial of the Hickam Three—Jim Albertini, Chuck Giuli, and myself, three members of catholic Action who had been indicted for conspiracy and destruction of government property (bearing a maximum penalty of 15 years and $10,000), for the pouring of our blood on top-secret files at Pacific Air Force Headquarters, Hickam Air Base. Our trial was to begin on August 8. At the beginning of July we faced a pre-trial hearing with Judge Martin Pence on several motions. We considered the granting of two of these motions as indispensable to the presentation of our trial defense.

The first was a motion of discovery, which asked that we be permitted to examine the evidence against us, the bloodied files, because this same evidence which the Government was using to prosecute us was our evidence in defense of our action. The files could be shown to contain evidence of the U.S. Air Force's use of anti-personnel weapons, designed for civilians, thereby violating both international law and the U.S. Constitution (Article VI, Section 2 of which makes all treaties signed by the U.S. Government, including the Geneva and Hague Conventions on the rights of civilians, the supreme law of the land).

Our second important motion asked that the court acknowledge our right to use international law in our defense. Otherwise the trial would be a legal farce. No one denied the action of pouring blood on the files. The question at issue was whether or not the action was legally justified, as could be determined by the files' contents and the laws applicable to them. Our contention was that the action was justified because it was done in order to draw attention to and hinder an enormous crime against life, defined clearly by international treaties incorporated into the U.S. Constitution.

From attending numerous resistance trials on the Mainland, and a beginning knowledge of how U.S. courts work, I knew that neither of these motions would be granted. American judges had always made their rulings so as to avoid in court the issue of the war in Indochina, no matter how obviously it was the central legal issue underlying an act of civil disobedience. This had occurred in the trials of hundreds of draft resisters and draft-board raiders whose civil disobedience was similar to our own. It was true that our action was unprecedented in having penetrated Air Force security to strike at files uniquely involved in U.S. war crimes, thereby raising the legal issue of war more directly than had ever been done before. We therefore had the clearest claim possible to raise the issue of the war in our defense. But we knew well that Judge Martin Pence, the most authoritarian judge in Hawaii (itself the most militarized of states), was not about to confront the U.S. Government for its war crimes on behalf of the Hickam Three. He would rule against us in the motions, and then having deprived us of any defense, would keep us under tight rein in a short trial to minimize public exposure to the issues.

The question before us was how to acknowledge and respond to the reality of this situation: As American war resisters we were particularly isolated. On the most heavily militarized island in the Pacific, where the military vies with tourism as Hawaii's major source of income, we could count on little local support in our trial. We were remote from Mainland movement support and press coverage. We faced a judge who bore down hard on anti-war defendants and presided over a strict court. And the only courtroom defense which could raise effectively the values of life and law for which we had acted, and now faced long sentences, was about to be taken from us a month before the trial.

There was no tactical way out of the reality which faced us. But there was one way to act on the same truth for which we had acted in pouring our blood, and that was to stand our ground. We knew what real moral and legal truths were at issue in our trial, and fortunately because of our knowledge of American courts, we knew the injustice which was already happening to us—and would happen quickly with our cooperation, unless we refused to give it. We could stand our ground and hold on to the truth regardless of the consequences, or we could consent in silence to the court's removal of that truth.

Non-cooperation with Judge Pence raised only one prospect:

immediate contempt of court and confinement until the day of our trial, one month away. For Shelley and me the prospect of a sudden jailing was especially critical. Shelley was taking a heavy load of summer school courses to help her prepare for a job to support herself and the children once I went to prison. My help with the children at this time was indispensable to her preparation for the post-trial imprisonment we already faced. We were also both heavily involved, she as head of the Defense Committee and I as a defendant, in pre-trial preparations which had not gone very far. Most important, in terms of the emotional weight of the moment, we were using the one month we thought we had left together to prepare ourselves personally for a long prison separation.

The decision we made, in a very real darkness, was that if in ruling on the motions the judge failed to grant us our defense, we would *both* refuse to cooperate in court. The only basis we had for our decision is that it was right to do it. Jim and Chuck had reached the same decision. When we shared that decision with the other members of catholic Action, they joined in it. We contacted all our known supporters in Hawaii urging them to join us at the pre-trial motions and to come prepared for resistance. Many of them did, enough to fill the courtroom to overflowing so that additional spectators were allowed that day to sit in the empty jurors' box.

Judge Pence treated us as expected. At first he tried to cut off our arguments, talking over Jim and me who were acting as our own attorneys. We argued our right to speak, a point the judge finally conceded. He settled back and listened to us for an hour, while we spoke from notes on the strictly legal issues we were standing on. We said we would not cooperate with the court if these laws and rights of evidence were not recognized. At that point he asked quickly what we meant, and we said that would become clear. When our arguments were finished, Judge Pence paused, then began denying all our motions in a prepared statement which said that our moral convictions (which we had avoided mentioning) were irrelevant to the strictly legal issues involved. I stood and began to ask the judge if he would reply to the arguments we had in fact made. He ordered me ejected from the courtroom, and I was taken by marshals to a cell in the rear of the building. Jim and Chuck also spoke up and were ejected. Then Shelley and others came forward to speak to the judge. They, too, were ejected. Finally, in a virtually empty courtroom, Judge Pence finished denying our motions and apparently wiped out our trial defense.

But for unknown reasons the judge cited none of us for contempt of court. I was released from my cell when the hearing was over. Our group got together again, recognized that the judge had denied our truth, and decided to hold on to it all the more in the upcoming trial. We would prepare for the trial just as if the court were open to the law. We would bring to Honolulu experts in international law and special witnesses on U.S. war crimes. If the judge denied them the right to take the stand, as would surely be the case, we would simply rest our case in court and hold our own trial outside.

In the meantime, we picketed and kept vigil daily outside the courthouse demanding a fair trial. I wrote an article citing the legal bases for our actions, denied by the judge, which was published in Honolulu's morning paper. Jim Albertini and I went on an evening radio program and dramatized the transcript of our pre-trial hearing, Jim playing himself and I Judge Pence. Shelley wrote a personal letter to Judge Pence telling him that she would be fasting until the trial as a prayer for a change of spirit in the courtroom. We met with members of the First Unitarian Church, the ACLU, the American Friends Service Committee, and the University of Hawaii Campus Ministry, who agreed to co-sponsor a week-long symposium at the University featuring all our trial witnesses. We contacted by phone two former prosecuting attorneys at the Nuremberg War Crimes Tribunal, Mary Kaufman and Benjamin Ferencz, who agreed to work with us as co-counsel at the trial. Further contacts were made with experts on anti-personnel weapons and on Laotian refugees from American bombing, who also agreed to come. Father Daniel Berrigan, whose 1968 trial in Baltimore I had attended so as to be a witness, said he would come to be a witness at ours. These trial plans were conveyed to the Honolulu papers which reported them amid speculation as to what would happen when Judge Pence refused to allow our witnesses to speak in court.

We prepared for that prospect by recognizing first that the mass bombing of the people of Indochina had in fact intensified since our blood-pouring action at Pacific Air Force Headquarters. If the court refused even to consider that paramount issue, on the final day of our trial members of our group would underline its seriousness by repeating the blood-pouring action at another military headquarters in Honolulu.

Three days before the trial was to begin, when our witnesses had already begun to arrive and public interest was building, we were informed that Judge Pence had withdrawn from the case. He gave no reasons. He was replaced by a younger man, Judge Samuel King, who had just been appointed as a federal judge in Hawaii. Ours was his first case.

Judge King allowed all our witnesses to testify. Hundreds of spectators heard what Nuremberg lawyer Mary Kaufman called the most startling testimony ever given in a U.S. courtroom on the war in Indochina. It included the sworn testimony of a former Air Force sergeant who said that while he was stationed at Hickam Air Base he had witnessed the deliberate targeting of a Laotian hospital for obliteration bombing, as well as the targeting of numerous other civilian objectives. Our trial was given headline media coverage in Honolulu for the week it was in progress, in spite of Hawaii's militarism. The symposium led by our witnesses at the University of Hawaii, in an auditorium packed every night, received an audience response whose intensity Dan Berrigan said he would never forget.

So far as the defendants' fate went, the charges against Chuck Giuli were dropped for lack of evidence. The bloodied files were required as courtroom evidence. Because the Pentagon refused to let anyone see them, the felony charges against Jim and me were reduced to misdemeanors. We were found guilty, sentenced to a year's probation, which we refused to cooperate with, and fined $500 each, which we refused to pay.

The point of this story is a force of truth which was realized gradually by holding on to that truth in spite of an apparently futile situation. That truth-force had deeper sources than any of the details I have mentioned, which barely describe its surface. The members of our group only created the conditions which allowed that force to surface in the Honolulu community. We acted as if the truth existed, and learned in the process of acting the truth out that it had a radically powerful existence. On the other hand, it was not simply a pragmatic power of our own making whose effects we could predict or control with any certainty. It is easy to imagine the self-destruction we would have experienced had we attempted simply to create a force to overcome the United States Government in a resistance trial in Honolulu: From such dreams come the bombs of Weatherpeople. The hypothesis of this essay is that in fact the transforming reality of such a force already existed, beyond our powers of creation. By acting as if it existed, by holding on to the truth as we knew it in spite of its futility, we witnessed the transformation of that truth into an objective force which acted autonomously and with surprising power on a wider community. It was a minor experiment in the transformation hypothesis, which gave evidence of an objective reality for change.

I believe the transforming reality we experienced in our trial came through a more deeply personal process than our firm resolution to hold on to the truth in court, though that was the immediate condition for transformation. It is necessary to speak of a more personal and more painful struggle for truth, without which no public force of truth comes into being. In my own case, that personal struggle linked the Hickam Three trial closely to an experience three years earlier.

In September 1969, I began a year of teaching at the University of Notre Dame in a nonviolence program. I knew that deep changes were necessary for a genuine spirit of nonviolence to grow or even survive on that campus. Nevertheless I had great hope, which was expressed in a self-created vision during a visit to the Notre Dame campus the preceding spring: While standing on the lawn beside Notre Dame's towering library with its mosaic mural of Christ reaching into the sky, I envisioned a Resistance Mass. I saw thousands of students spread out on the lawn participating in a Mass, celebrated by priests against the backdrop of the Christ figure, in which the Offertory prayer would be the spiritually revolutionary one of students and professors bringing forward and destroying their draft cards—a Mass in genuine remembrance of Christ, offering resistance and sacrifice in response to the violence of America in Indochina.

On October 15, 1969, in Notre Dame's observance of the national moratorium against the war, the vision became real. On that afternoon, in a Mass on the library lawn attended by the Notre Dame and St. Mary's College student bodies and faculties, five students and two professors did come forward at the Offertory. We tore our draft cards in two and placed them in a chalice held by visiting British Archbishop T.D. Roberts while an FBI photographer snapped pictures a few feet away. (Because, I believe, of the surprisingly strong support given us by the Notre Dame community in a liturgical setting, the Government took no further action other than a few FBI phone calls and attempted visits.) The Mass was an overpoweringly beautiful experience of community, and a promising beginning for our program.

But my hope of initiating nonviolent changes at Notre Dame, a deeply egocentric perspective from the beginning, collapsed soon after when Shelley and I met and committed our lives to each other in spite of the fact that each of us was married to another person. Shelley was clear in conscience from the beginning that her marriage was invalid. I was less clear concerning mine, though I should have been the opposite, and for months vacillated between questions of my own (non-existent) purity and reputation and recognizing the more difficult truths of a new way and life. I could not recognize and live the truth because I was unwilling to let go of a false image of myself, that of a would-be saint for whom divorce and re-marriage were not thinkable. The winter and spring which followed at Notre Dame were a step-by-step involuntary experience of Gandhi's nonviolent principle, that of being reduced to nothing, in a far more humbling way than envisioned in any of my nonviolent scenarios, and which culminated in a sense of spiritual destruction. I experienced my personal emptiness in a way I will never forget. Nor will I ever forget the grace and strength of the people who helped then, beginning with Shelley and an extraordinary Holy Cross priest, Father David Burrell, whose love and wisdom went deeper than any judgment of my mistakes. From them I learned more about nonviolence than I had ever known in a self which felt itself a redeemer of others. My year at Notre Dame initiated no nonviolent changes in that institution but instead revealed the source of obstacles to change as my own shadowed self.

I believe from that year's experience that he who decides to lose his life in order to find it in a calculated way will get smashed by Reality. On the other hand, it is that ultimate degree of losing any control over Reality (involuntary in my case) which can lay the foundation for a growth in truth. We learn to live "Not my will but thine be done" in the experience of total darkness. My preparation for the requirements in truth of the Honolulu trial began in a very real way at Notre Dame, at that point where the personal loss was total.

To return from my own darkness, to the truth of Jesus, we can say that if the truth of Jesus lay in what he became, an objective force of truth and love, then the "greater works" Jesus prophesies in John's Gospel lie in a similar direction of becoming. And to return to Jung's observation regarding the Christ-symbol as understood (or misunderstood) today, we can also say that Jesus' particular way of becoming, one lost to us behind the final, objective force of his truth presented in the Gospels, may have been significantly different from the way we imagine it—in fact, must have been if Jung's insight regarding the nature of the human psyche is correct.

A key to Jung's model of the psyche is "the shadow." The shadow is the sum of everything I refuse to acknowledge about myself. It is my unconscious self. Because of an incompatibility with my consciously chosen attitude, the elements of the shadow are denied expression in conscious life and coalesce into a relatively autonomous psychic reality with contrary tendencies in the unconscious. By now it is well known that to the extent that the ego ignores the shadow elements of the psyche, or forces them to remain repressed and unacknowledged in the unconscious, it is inviting destruction into the world. The shadow can bring destruction when it reacts autonomously and surfaces unexpectedly. Jung has identified not only personal self-destruction but the collective evils of modern totalitarianism with autonomous eruptions of the shadow. On the other hand, if a person can acknowledge the shadow and thus make it conscious, that person can become whole and a source of great psychic energy. S(he) will have emerged from self-division into a whole expression of her own truth. The personal goal of Jung's process evokes Gandhi's description of the "satyagrahi," or person of truth-force.

Jung states that the process of making the shadow conscious, while beginning to resolve a dangerous tension between conscious and unconscious, causes at first a conscious cleavage and tension of opposites (conscious attitude over against shadow) which in turn seek compensation in unity. The adjustment is achieved through symbols, in a further process whose nature and symbolic power absorbed Jung in the final years of his life:

> The conflict between the opposites can strain our psyche to the breaking point, if we take them seriously, or if they take us seriously. The *tertium non datur* of logic proves its worth: no solution can be seen. If all goes well, the solution, seemingly of its own accord, appears out of nature. Then and then only is it convincing. It is felt as grace. Since the solution proceeds out of the confrontation and clash of opposites, it is usually an unfathomable mixture of conscious and unconscious factors, and therefore a symbol, a coin split into two halves which fit together precisely. It represents the result of the joint labors of consciousness

and the unconscious, and attains the likeness of the God-image
in the form of the mandala, which is probably the simplest model
of a concept of wholeness, and one which spontaneously arises in
the mind as a representation of the struggle and reconciliation of
opposites. The clash, which is at first of a purely personal nature,
is soon followed by the insight that the subject conflict is only a
single instance of the universal conflict of opposites. Our psyche
is set up in accord with the structure of the universe, and what
happens in the macrocosm likewise happens in the infinitesimal
and most subjective reaches of the psyche. [7]

The "God-image" is a term Jung derived from the Church
Fathers, according to whom the image of God is imprinted on the
human soul. Jung regarded such an image, when spontaneously
produced in the mandala, as being from the psychological point of
view a symbol of the Self, of psychic wholeness. He suggests at
numerous points in his work that the Self itself, an unfathomable
reality which embraces both conscious and unconscious, may coincide
ultimately with what has always been referred to as "God". Our
experience of the Self, just as our experience of God, is always a
defeat for the ego. Jung saw the psyche as an opening to an
inexhaustible reality. His concept of self-realization, in a Western
psychological context, corresponded in an extraordinary way to
Hindu and Buddhist doctrines.

The crucial, personal process of acknowledging the shadow
therefore initiates a conscious tension of opposites, and finally
through their strain and confrontation, the graceful production of
symbols of unity—a unity deriving from the reality of the Self or of
God.

The Gospel of Luke tells us that Jesus when he was increasingly
besieged by crowds would always go off to some place where he could
be alone and pray (Luke 5:16). This recurring retreat into solitude
repeats Jesus' preliminary to his public life, his forty days in the
wilderness. A question worth re-opening is the nature of Jesus'
experience in solitude and in the wilderness.

The wilderness exposes one to the experience of powerlessness,
to a sense of absolute dependence on forces beyond oneself. One goes
into the solitude of the wilderness to pray because it shatters
self-sufficient pride and forces one to acknowledge whatever can
remain hidden elsewhere. The wilderness can kill, with a speed and

power which is startling when realized. I have thought of this power in my home in the interior of British Columbia, really only the edge of the wilderness but where people who respect its power too little often die quickly. The Judean wilderness which Jesus went into, a desert waste where no human being can live without water for more than a few hours, was an especially urgent reminder of individual powerlessness and emptiness.

In the earliest account (Mark 1:12-13), we are told simply that immediately after Jesus' baptism by John, "the Spirit drove him out into the wilderness and he remained there for forty days, and was tempted by Satan. He was with the wild beasts, and the angels looked after him." Mark says no more. Matthew and Luke elaborate on the nature of the temptations, each of them being a form of messianic power: economic (bread to the hungry), political (all the kingdoms of the world), and spiritual (triumphal religious authority over the people). Jesus rejected the temptations, then left the wilderness for Galilee where he began his public life by proclaiming the kingdom of God.

In terms of the Jungian model of the human psyche, which, if accurate, was shared by the man Jesus, Jesus' wilderness experience would have involved his acknowledgment of the shadow. More than that, if we are to judge by the power and wholeness of Jesus' truth of the kingdom after he came out of the wilderness, his encounter with the emptiness of his shadow must have been an inconceivably ego-shattering experience. For it was from the liberating depths of such an experience that the kingdom of God was first proclaimed with power, and lived by Jesus, amid periodic retreats into solitude, to the ultimate truths of the Gospel: death and resurrection.

The shadow is what I *am* but will not admit I am. For the shadow of the psyche involves me in a deepening self-recognition which is more humiliating and emptying than the normal limits of endurance. In the end, acknowledging the shadow means acknowledging a bottomless void within me. The initial question of truth-force is: How deeply will I acknowledge my own emptiness?

Jesus acknowledged his temptations as real. Our way of looking at that normally is to view it as an external operation, with Jesus and Satan engaged in a morality play in the desert. Jung's model of the psyche suggests a profoundly internal interpretation of the text. It suggests that the temptations came from within Jesus and involved him in a deeply interior act of self-recognition. Jung's model suggests that in rejecting Satan's temptations in the wilderness, Jesus would at the same time have recognized himself in those very forces—the drives toward messianic power in its political, spiritual, and economic forms. New Testament scholars have become increasingly aware of Jesus' living in a context of violent revolutionary activity, in which the Zealot political-religious ideal of overthrowing the Roman occupying forces in a holy war was close to the hearts of most Jews, especially the poor. By acknowledging himself in those collective forces to the point of recognizing his will to personify them, yet rejecting their ideal of power as satanic, Jesus would have been free to open himself to a deeper Reality and to proclaim a kingdom of God rather than his own: "Not my will but thine be done."

We need to reflect here on the psychic fact that to go so deep as to acknowledge the personal roots of a desire for power, which will be seen to rest ultimately on one's own impotence and nothingness, is an experience of overwhelming darkness. There is nothing darker in the psyche than the shadow of power-seeking. Jesus' temptations are recalled by the evangelists as having been temptations to an enormous power ("all the kingdoms of the world"). It is difficult to imagine Jesus undergoing such temptations alone in the Judean wilderness, in the situation of ultimate powerlessness, without his finally acknowledging their roots in his own emptiness, thus plunging into a psychic night.

The nature of Jesus' experience in the wilderness can be viewed backward from the later Christian proclamation that Jesus died for the sins of all, that all might become free. The question can be raised: Did Jesus in his temptations to power acknowledge a shadow in himself which went to an inconceivable depth, and thus issued finally in a universal light—his identification with the sins and suffering of all, to the point of accepting personal responsibility for them?

In *The Brothers Karamazov*, the saintly monk Zossima states salvation in these terms:

> There is only one means of salvation, then take yourself and make yourself responsible for all men's sins, that is the truth, you know, friends, for as soon as you sincerely make yourself responsible for everything and for all men, you will see at once that it is really so, and that you are to blame for every one and for all things. But throwing your own indolence and impotence on others you will end by sharing the pride of Satan and murmuring against God. [8]

It is really so: Each of us is to blame for everyone and for all things. The nature of personal responsibility is such that when faced in the psychic depths of Reality, in a shadow common to us all, that responsibility encompasses all of humankind. Each person is to blame for everyone and for all things.

Gandhi put it simply:

Whenever I see an erring man, I say to myself, I have also erred; when I see a lustful man, I say to myself, so was I once; and in this way I feel kinship with every one in the world and feel that I cannot be happy without the humblest of us being happy.[9]

The transformation hypothesis assumes that every living person is in touch with the same shadow and the same Reality of Oneness as were Jesus and Gandhi. Along a way of darkness we begin to sense the oneness hinted at through the shadow of the unconscious self. It is my individual consciousness with its pride and pretended control over Reality which keeps me from being present to the possibility of the one world in truth. That possibility is always there, through my shadow and its emptiness. Transformation begins as a question of presence, my being present to pain, my own and others. Through experiments in Reality the possibility of the one world begins to be sensed because one is moving along a way of faith and darkness. Faith and its experiments beyond the ego open us to a transforming Reality. By entering the shadow and the darkness, by thus beginning to become one in our own truth, we sense the possible oneness of the world.

The nature of this oneness has been described by Gandhi's secretary and biographer, Pyarelal:

Individual psyches have been likened to innumerable coral reefs widely separated each from the other by the circumambient ocean but all united with one another at the base on the ocean floor from which they are sprung. The achievement of soul force depends on re-establishing our unity consciously with all psyches which manifestly exists beneath the threshold of individual consciousness and communicating that experience to others.[10]

Gandhi believed in *advaita*, in the essential unity of humanity and of all that lives. He believed that if one person gains spiritually, the whole world gains with her and, if one person falls, the whole world falls to that extent. The psychic foundation of Gandhi's techniques of *satyagraha*, of truth-force or soul-force, is the union of all individual psyches in an unconscious Self, which Jung says is experienced as God and which Gandhi says *is* God.

It is this unifying Self of a collective unconscious which can be hypothesized as the unexplored source of an inconceivable energy for change—the psychic equivalent of Einstein's $E = mc^2$.

"The coming of the Son of Man will be like lightning striking in the east and flashing far into the west."

The image Jesus gave for the victory of Truth in history is one of brilliant energy, horizon to horizon—an image like nothing so much as a nuclear blast in the sky, yet symbolizing a different form of energy. Unlike many followers of Christ, Gandhi understood Jesus' image of the kingdom in a profoundly psychic sense, a kingdom of Reality opening one to an inner universe "governed by laws that are as immutable, as self-sanctioning and capable of as precise and objective a handling as, for instance, the laws of motion that govern the world of matter."[11] The energy of our inner universe is more powerful than nuclear energy but because its science has been neglected it lies dormant within us. This unconscious, psychic energy has at its core a principle which Gandhi experienced as self-acting, as we did in a minor way in the Hickam Three trial. It is an autonomous energy for transformation which when opened up—by our holding on to the truth as we know it, and ultimately surrendering our lives to that truth in darkness—surfaces in the world as an overpowering force of truth and love, limited only by the individual's degree of unwillingness to let go and become one with it. In this respect Gandhi compared the individual to a drop, and the energy within her to an ocean, that ocean of energy which is humanity, Self, and God:

> If we shatter the chains of egotism and melt into the ocean of humanity, we share its majesty. To feel that we are something is to set up a barrier between God and ourselves; to cease feeling that we are something is to become one with God. A drop in the ocean partakes of the greatness of its parent, although it is unconscious of it. But it is dried up as soon as it enters upon an existence independent of the ocean.[12]

This self-acting energy of Reality is unconscious to us. The way into it is through a self-sacrificial union. The individual psyche realizes soul-force, an overwhelming force of wholeness in the world, only when it has re-established a conscious unity with all psyches and has expressed that experience to the world.

The kingdom of Reality will be like lightning striking in the east and flashing far into the west when that hidden, latent energy of the unconscious Self which is God and humanity has been opened by sacrifice and allowed to surface into a conscious flash of truth, a force of oneness manifested in a spiritual chain reaction of which we already have examples: the effect of Jesus as Christ on the empire which crucified him, the power of Gandhi as soul-force over the empire which jailed him and the warring factions which killed him. Lightning east to west will be the widening practical realization in an end-time of the meaning of Jesus' and Gandhi's revolutions, and the consequent, surfacing truth-force and love-force of a finally conscious oneness, a progressive re-uniting of individual psyches in an expression of inconceivable energy.

What is being hypothesized as a way of psychic transformation can be stated further through its physical analogue: a nuclear explosion.

Our concern here is with the atomic bomb's matter-to-energy transformation, the way in which an inconceivable power is released from extraordinarily small pieces of matter—about the size of a baseball in the case of the uranium or plutonium which is the A-bomb material.[13] The atomic weapon is in fact essentially nothing more than its ball of uranium-235 or plutonium-239. When either of these elements has been sufficiently purified, it need only be assembled in a large enough quantity, "the critical mass," for it to set off automatically an instantaneous chain reaction. The assembly is accomplished quickly in the bomb by shooting one sub-critical mass into the other so as to exceed the explosive size. Overall, it is simply by purification and integration (of its smaller-than-critical parts) that a handful of uranium becomes a force equal to 20,000 tons of TNT.

The A-bomb process illustrates a self-acting energy in matter whose power covers the world. As the uranium is purified and concentrated for its use in the bomb, it remains matter but edges closer and closer to that critical mass at which point its earth-shattering energy will suddenly and overwhelmingly take over. This enormous degree of energy exists in every particle of matter, as Einstein showed. In a very real sense, a power to reach the sky exists in the table on which I am now writing, though its energy will probably never be released. It is not the right kind of substance for any known way of conversion. But more to the point here, for the horizon-spanning energy of even uranium to take over from its handful of matter, a painstaking process of purification is first necessary.

It is the equivalent degree of autonomous psychic energy which Gandhi postulated in every living person as the basis of truth-force. The degree of energy for transformation present in our psychic or spiritual reality is normally as unimaginable as the energy in a sub-critical mass. Moreover, to reach the critical point of a spiritual transformation in humanity, where an autonomous Reality might take over and fill the horizon, would require an even more painstaking process of purification in the person or community seeking that realization, because its possibility has been so little explored. Gandhi spoke simply on the means of such a purification: 1) through a form of being in prayer in which the person becomes ever-more-one with Reality in an inner wholeness; 2) through a form of being through service in which the person becomes ever-more-one with Reality in a communal wholeness. "You must love the Lord your God with all your heart, with all your soul, and with all your mind. This is the greatest and the first commandment. The second resembles it: You must love your neighbour as yourself." (Matthew 22:37-9) In the fulfilling of both commandments, at a depth virtually unknown to us, one is remembering and re-establishing in action and conscious unity that forgotten psychic oneness of all life in the depths of the world which Jung characterized as the experience of God. In such a way, through prayer and service at a depth of ultimate sacrifice, a community of satyagrahis will create the conditions of that critical spirit in which a self-acting energy of truth and love can transform a whole society.

But to sense so far-reaching a possibility it is necessary to hold on with one's life to the very limited truth already seen. Each person has her truth, but it is rare in a morally paralyzed society to see a person holding on to that truth—which one must be willing to die for rather than relinquish, in order to grow in the living Reality of which it is a part. What is recognized as the truth must be lived beyond anything we may have thought possible if it is to approach the critical spirit of a transforming energy.

The atomic bomb is still one step short, though, of the most powerful manifestation on earth of Einstein's matter-to-energy formula, the thermonuclear or hydrogen bomb. The H-bomb's composition consists of two parts: The first is an A-bomb core, identical with the un-assembled uranium ball described above but used in the H-bomb as a triggering device. The chain reaction of the core bomb will create the over 100 million degrees of heat necessary to convert the outer shell of the H-bomb, solid hydrogen, into a roaring fireball with 1,000 or more times the power of the bomb which destroyed Hiroshima. Within this fireball are billions of billions of billions of hydrogen atoms which have come together, or fused, into combinations of a new element, helium. Triggered by the autonomous energy and heat from the purified core substance, the thermonuclear fireball is a massive union of atoms comprising a new substance.

The analogy of the H-bomb can bring out the final character of a countering psychic energy for transformation, lightning east to west. The exact opposite of the H-bomb's destructive purpose, but psychic equivalent of its energy, is the kingdom of Reality which would be the final victory of Truth in history—a force of truth and love powerful enough to fuse billions of individual psyches into a global realization of essential oneness. The experience of such a spiritual force of fusion is unimaginable, and the mere hypothesizing of it, as in this book, as a psychic and historical possibility will go beyond any but the most willing suspension of disbelief. But there is no reason why the same psyche which, when turned outward, was able to create the conditions for a self-acting force of over 100 million degrees of heat, thus realizing an inconceivable thermonuclear fusion, cannot some day turn sufficiently inward to create the conditions for an equally inconceivable (but nature-balancing) fusion in its own psychic or spiritual reality. The main deterrent to its doing so is that sharp sense in us all of the conditions necessary for a self-sacrificing love corresponding in any way to the energy of a nuclear fireball. But an end-time can also be a beginning. The purpose of this book is to suggest a basis for hope provided we are willing to experiment in a transforming law of our inner being, that law of which Gandhi said:

> When the practice of the law becomes universal, God will reign on earth as God does in Heaven. Earth and Heaven are in us. We know the earth, and we are strangers to the Heaven within us. [14]

1 Richard Barnet, "Race Without Reason," *Sojourners* (February 1977), p. 8.

2 The basis for this statement, made in conversations with the writer, is found in Robert C. Aldridge, *The Counterforce Syndrome* (pamphlet published in 1978 by the Institute for Policy Studies, 1901 Q Street, N.W., Washington, D.C. 20009) and in Aldridge's book, *First Strike* published recently by South End Press. The date of a likely "point of no return" is relative to the progress or delay of particular first-strike weapons. Delays in the Trident and the MX, before the Reagan Administration began pushing them, moved the deadline for a turning point into the 80s.

3 C.G. Jung, *Aion* (Princeton University Press: 1959), p. 261.

4 C.G. Jung, *Psychology and Alchemy* (Princeton University Press: 1968), p. 19.

5 Jung, *Aion*, p. 42.

6 M.K. Gandhi, *All Men Are Brothers* (Ahmedabad, Navajivan Publishing House: 1960), pp. 60-1.

7 C.G. Jung, *Memories, Dreams, Reflections* (Vintage: 1963), p. 335.

8 Fyodor Dostoevsky, *The Brothers Karamazov* tr. Constance Garnett (Modern Library: 1950), p. 384.

9 Pyarelal, *Mahatma Gandhi: The last Phase, Volume II* (Ahmedabad, Navajivan Publishing House: 1958), p. 792.

10 *loc.sit.*

11 Pyarelal, p. 791.

12 Pyarelal, p. 789.

13 Books consulted for information on nuclear weapons include: Selig Hecht, *Explaining the Atom* (Viking: 1947); Robert Macaulay, *The World of Energy* (Toronto, Newton Publishing Co.: 1961); Ralph E. Lapp, *Atoms and People* (Harper: 1956).

14 Pyarelal, p. 791. I have replaced Gandhi's "He" referring back to God with a second use of "God."

3
The Kingdom is the World in Reality

The world of nuclear proliferation, the world of global poverty and famine, the world of big-power imperialism and third-world nationalism, the world with a constant undercurrent of mistrust, exploitation, and mutual violence, a violence due to consume the earth, is a world which offers no hope to humanity. Yet that world is at the center of the consciousness of anyone concerned with justice and peace, for that is the world which needs to undergo change, or rather a radical transformation, in order for justice and peace to become real. That world, which will either be transformed or destroy itself, is overwhelming to a person's consciousness. Thus the very reasonable anxiety which the world induces in our minds, and the haste (of those who have the means to do so) to simply forget it. For those of us who are unable to forget the world and instead wish to change it, we experience the truth that the world is too much with us. The world is too much with us in our eyes and hearts and souls, the world is too overwhelming to our consciousness and too deep in our spirits for us to see and live a way of radical transformation.

The seemingly hopeless question of the nonviolent transformation of so overwhelming a world suggests the need for a perspective in which the world is less with us, yet a perspective which must be just as real as nuclear stockpiles and starving children.

To illustrate this: Our house in Hedley, British Columbia, stands under Stemwinder Mountain, which is a sheer rock slide and cliff reaching 3,000 feet into the sky above us. The loose shale of the slide area covers most of this height and is topped by a series of rocky ledges with patches of grass and pine trees growing at dizzying angles. When we gaze at these heights, we can spot tiny white specks moving slowly across them, mountain goats climbing far above our town.

One day my two oldest sons and I decided to climb Stemwinder Mountain. We didn't try to scale the cliff, which is too sheer for us, but chose a route around the side where several big hills leading one into another serve as stepping stones up the mountain. After we had climbed over the hills and lost sight of the town and valley below, we reached a high grassy knoll with a few pine trees. Uncertain where we were, we walked across the knoll to a line where the grass and trees seemed to stop. We looked out, and directly below us 3,000 feet down was a row of tiny squares, one of which was our house.

What we were given in that moment, when we unexpectedly looked down the sheer cliff at our town below, was an entirely new perspective. We saw the tiny character of our house from the standpoint of the goats who looked down on us every day, and we saw and felt beneath our feet the latent energy of a tower of earth which could at any time slide down and bury the specks of life below. We experienced the reality of our town from an entirely new perspective.

For us who live and suffer in the world, there seems to be no point outside the world from which to view it and our efforts at nonviolent transformation in an entirely new perspective. The question itself seems at least as overwhelming as the sheer face of a 3,000-foot cliff. But perhaps within our own experience and the experience of others there are a few clues toward a now-inconceivable perspective, or in the analogy of Stemwinder Mountain, a few hills to serve as stepping stones toward a perspective on the world unknown to our lives where they stand now.

Gandhi's beliefs on nonviolent truth-force provide one such clue. Because they were acted on as hypotheses by Gandhi, and tested by a series of living experiments as strict in their methods as any laboratory analysis, Gandhi's beliefs became operating principles ever more deeply grounded in his life. Gandhi's radical belief in the power of nonviolence through oneness is of particular importance here.

His statement of that belief which is probably most scandalous to our sense of reality was given by Gandhi in response to a question a few hours before he was killed. Gandhi was asked then, by an American journalist, how he would meet the atomic bomb—with non violence? He said:

> I will not go underground. I will not go into shelter. I will come out in the open and let the pilot see I have not a trace of ill-will against him. The pilot will not see our faces from his great height, I know. But the longing in our hearts—that he will not come to harm—would reach up to him and his eyes would be opened.[1]

Gandhi declared further that a single silent thought can envelop the whole world, but he also said that no person in the flesh had ever succeeded in expressing such a thought fully in word or in action.[2] The basis of this faith in the ultimate transforming power of nonviolence was Gandhi's view of the absolute oneness of God and of humanity:

> I believe in the absolute oneness of God and, therefore, of humanity. What though we have many beliefs? We have but one soul. The rays of the sun are many through refraction. But they have the same source. I cannot, therefore, detach myself from the wickedest soul nor may I be denied identity with the most virtuous.[3]

Gandhi's operating belief in the power of nonviolence through a fundamental oneness of reality offers one clue toward a perspective on the world.

From a psychic perspective different from Gandhi's, C.G. Jung also investigated and conducted experiments in the power of an underlying oneness of reality. Jung's investigations resulted in the formulation of his theory of Synchronicity.

By "Synchronicity" Jung meant simply the occurrence of a meaningful coincidence in time. He defined a synchronistic phenomenon more precisely as either the meaningful coincidence of a psychic state and a physical event which have no causal relationship to one another, or the meaningful coincidence of similar thoughts or dreams occurring at the same time in different places.

For example, Jung in describing a series of synchronistic events in his autobiography, *Memories, Dreams, Reflections*, recounts one such incident involving a patient with whom he had lost contact and who in the meantime had relapsed into a serious depression. One night after delivering a lecture Jung returned late to his hotel and went to bed where he lay awake restlessly a long time. Then, after finally falling asleep, he awoke with a start at about two o'clock, and had the distinct impression that someone had opened the door hastily and come into the room. He continues:

> I instantly turned on the light, but there was nothing. Someone might have mistaken the door, I thought, and I looked into the corridor. But it was still as death. "Odd," I thought, "someone did come into the room!" Then I tried to recall exactly what had happened, and it occurred to me that I had been awakened by a

feeling of dull pain, as though something had struck my forehead and then the back of my skull. The following day I received a telegram saying that my patient had committed suicide. He had shot himself. Later, I learned that the bullet had come to rest in the back wall of the skull. [4]

Causality cannot explain synchronistic phenomena. Jung believed they were connected primarily with activated archetypal processes in the unconscious, a collective unconscious common to all—the foundation of what the ancients called the "sympathy of all things."

Jung proposed Synchronicity as a principle of meaning in reality which exists outside cause and effect, yet governs the universe in a comprehensive way. Synchronicity was in a sense Jung's psychic equivalent of the Relativity theory of his friend Einstein, for in Synchronicity as in Relativity the subjective condition of the observer is a primary factor in the relativity of space and time—whose distances and gaps are nullified in a meaningful way in relation to a particular psyche, as in Jung's experience of the death of his patient. [5]

A forerunner of Synchronicity is the Tao, that Principle or Way of Meaning in the universe which can never be spoken yet runs through the center of existence and can silently guide one's every step toward a profound unity and harmony. Synchronicity focuses on the psyche as our personal key to the Way of Meaning, inasmuch as the psyche by its attitude and actions can harmonize itself both inwardly and outwardly in symbols of unity, or synchronistic events. The experiencing of that revealed oneness becomes possible for a psyche which has undergone an *abaissement*, a lowering of the mental level and at bottom the humiliation of its assumed ego-centered control over reality. [6]

A personal example of this took place in the Fall of 1972, following the trial in Honolulu which resulted in Jim Albertini and me being sentenced to a $500 fine each and a year's probation for pouring blood on top-secret Air Force files. We refused to cooperate with our sentence, and as a first step in our noncooperation decided to go elsewhere than to the probation office at the time of our first probation appointments: Jim would go instead to Camp Smith in Hawaii to deliver a citizen's arrest warrant to the office of the Commander-in-Chief of the Pacific for his involvement in war crimes;

I would fly from Hawaii to Copenhagen to the hearings of the International Commission of Inquiry into U.S. War Crimes in Indochina, where I would present an initial payment of $200 of our fine money to Vietnamese witnesses and victims of the crime of U.S. bombing.

I arrived in Copenhagen with a sense of great expectancy and uncertainty. A member of the International Commission had invited me to the hearings, and I hoped that I would be able to speak out in Copenhagen as we had done at our trial on the war crimes we were resisting. The member of the Commission had said he thought I would be especially welcomed to the hearings as a witness who was a U.S. resister in violation of probation by my very presence there. Drawing on his encouragement, I felt I could make a unique contribution as an example of ongoing resistance. But his invitation was only a personal one, and I had to leave Honolulu for Copenhagen without having received the official invitation to the hearings which my friend said I could expect shortly. Nor had the official invitation come to Honolulu in the interval of my several days' travel, as Shelley told me in our phone conversations during this time. Thus the expectant yet uncertain mood of my arrival in Denmark.

In Copenhagen I discovered there was no invitation. The Commission member I knew was not there, and those in authority had little time to hear of my reasons for coming. In mercy to a would-be witness who had traveled half the way around the globe, they agreed finally to give me a hotel room and meal tickets but there was no interest in my testifying or contributing in any way to the work of the Commission. I was told that if I was lucky and there weren't too many witnesses I could keep the room and meal tickets for the full week of hearings.

It was in a state of personal humiliation, a result of the puncturing of my own ambitions in Copenhagen, that I then attended the war crimes hearings. And learned the real reason for my being there besides the delivery of our $200 to the Vietnamese: To learn as an American resister just how little I knew of the crimes I was resisting, and less still of the beauty of the people of Indochina, some of whom were there to speak of their agony. One of these spoke to me in a way which brought home as never before the reality of oneness in the world.

A final witness from Laos, Nang Oun Kham, was a small, shy, 18-year-old woman who had obvious difficulty walking to the front of the room and using her limbs. She spoke to the Commission through a translator, the shyness giving way then to a sudden sharp intensity in her Laotian words. She began by describing how in 1969 U.S. planes came often to bomb her village, demolishing homes and killing many of the people, including her father. After her father's death, she and her family moved and sought refuge in another village. Again they were bombed by the planes, and her brother, a monk, was killed while praying in a pagoda. Nang Oun Kham spoke through tears of seeing him lying dead in the pagoda with his stomach hanging out. Her mother was wounded also as the bombing raids continued. The family moved again, this time to a refuge deep in the jungle. And there the U.S. planes caught Nang Oun Kham herself: She said she was bombed and wounded seriously on March 2, 1972. In response to a question from the Commission, she repeated the precise date on which she had been bombed.

Afterwards I went up to Nang Oun Kham to respond to her testimony with word of a remarkable coincidence. I told her that on March 2, 1972, the day on which she was bombed by the United States Air Force in Laos, we in Hawaii had poured blood on top-secret air-war files in Pacific Air Force Headquarters, in a room where the bombing of Laos was targetted. She listened to those words through her translator with her eyes on mine in a deepening recognition which went across borders, languages, and the agony of Hawaii-to-Laos bombings. The beauty of her life, the pain in us all, the oneness of the world—they were all one in her face. She embraced me while I cried. She gave me a small pin to wear and take back to Hawaii, a flag of the Laotian Patriotic Front, in whose hospital she had been nursed back to what health she had left. She said the pin would be a symbol of the unity of her people and mine and of our common struggle toward a world of peace and justice.

The pin was finally lost and I have no pictures of Nang Oun Kham. But she remains deeply present, a presence of the kingdom of oneness which is the world in its innermost Reality.

The synchronicity of lives and events is a visible reminder of the oneness of God, humanity, and the universe, a reminder needed especially by an ego-centered psyche, which in my case had been forcibly broken down just enough by reality in Copenhagen to admit the grace-filled presence of Nang Oun Kham. But the reality seen in synchronicity, which is the Reality of the One, suggests the possibility of a profound voluntary entering on that Way in which unifying events will correspond to an ever-deepening inward surrender to the One. This is a way not of cause and effect but a complete absorption and acceptance of a world-embracing Reality whose transforming power is limited only by the disciple's lack of faith: "I tell you solemnly, if your faith were the size of a mustard seed you could say to this mountain, 'Move from here to there,' and it would move; nothing would be impossible for you." (Matthew 17:20)

The mountain to be moved is the world itself, and at an inconceivable depth of faith it can be moved to the point of transformation.

But Jesus was speaking to the point of view of disciples lacking in faith, and perhaps, from another standpoint, there is in reality nothing to be moved—but only a way to be followed, to the point of complete emptiness.

In an entry in his *Asian Journal* written less than a month before his death, Thomas Merton recounts his meeting in the Himalaya with the Tibetan Chatral Rimpoche, whom he describes as "the greatest rimpoche I have met so far and a very impressive person."[7] In the conversation which took place between the Christian monk from Gethsemani and the Tibetan spiritual master, who "looked like a vigorous old peasant in a Bhutanese jacket tied at the neck with thongs and a red woolen cap on his head," the talk covered all sorts of ground

> but all leading back to dzogchen, the ultimate emptiness, the unity of sunyata and karuna, going "beyond the dharmakaya" and "beyond God" to the ultimate perfect emptiness. He said he had meditated in solitude for thirty years or more and had not attained to perfect emptiness and I said I hadn't either.
>
> The unspoken or half-spoken message of the talk was our complete understanding of each other as people who were somehow *on the edge* of great realization and knew it and were trying, somehow or other, to go out and get lost in it—and that it was a grace for us to meet one another.[8]

We need to take seriously the belief of these two spiritual masters, from both East and West, that the deepest experience of reality is the ultimate perfect emptiness which they were on the edge of and needed to get lost in. For the nature of the supreme realization being sought by them, the ultimate perfect emptiness, is a classic description of reality from the standpoint of those few who have perceived reality from its very center. That description from the center must have something to say about our struggle to move the mountain of the world at the surface.

    Ramana Maharshi, a great Indian sage who lived in the first half of this century, said of the relation between the world and the individual, "As you are, so is the world." [9]

The ultimate perfect emptiness of reality suggests that the mountain of the world, and the struggle of the self to transform it, is in fact an illusion. The ultimate perfect emptiness suggests further that the illusion of struggling with the mountain is based on the ignorance of that ego in each of us which would like to regard itself as an identity separate from the world, as a separate identity which stands over against the objective mountain of suffering and injustice. But "as you are, so is the world." The mountain of the world with its overwhelming evil and suffering is not out there. That mountain is in here. The world in its deepest evil is in fact me.

    As Thomas Merton once put it in his essay, "Is 'the World' a Problem?",

for anyone who has seriously entered into the medieval Christian, or the Hindu, or the Buddhist conceptions of *contemptus mundi, Mara* and the *"emptiness of the world,"* it will be evident that this means not the rejection of reality, but the unmasking of an illusion. The world as pure object is something that is not there. It is not a reality outside us for which we exist. It is not a firm and absolute objective structure which has to be accepted on its own inexorable terms. The world has in fact no terms of its own. It dictates no terms to man. We and our world interpenetrate. If anything, the world exists for us, and we exist for ourselves. It is only in assuming full responsibility for our world, for our lives and for ourselves that we can be said to live really for God. The whole human reality, which of course transcends us as individuals and as a collectivity, nevertheless interpenetrates the world of nature (which is obviously "real") and the world of history (also "real" in so far as it is made up of the total effect of all our decisions and actions). But this reality, though "eternal" and "objective," is not something entirely independent of us, which dominates us inexorably from without through the medium of certain fixed laws which science alone can discover and use. It is an extension and a projection of ourselves and of our lives, and if we attend to it respectfully, while attending also to our own freedom and our own integrity, we can learn to obey its ways and coordinate our lives with its mysterious movements. The way to find the real "world" is not merely to measure and observe what is outside us, but to discover our own inner ground.

For that is where the world is, first of all; in my deepest self.[10]

Thomas Merton's and Ramana Maharshi's identification of the world with our innermost reality has been confirmed from another direction by the scientifically revolutionary worldview of modern physics. From a strictly scientific standpoint, we can clear our eyes of that habitual blindness which defines the world as an object beyond the self, by recalling that modern physics has exploded the myth of the commonsense perception of the world as a solid, tangible mass existing by itself.

Atomic physics revealed each object in the world as consisting almost entirely of empty space, a nothingness broken only by unimaginably tiny specks of electrons, whirling around their nuclei but separated from them by distances a hundred thousand times their own size.[11] But as quantum physics further revealed, even in searching through the vast emptiness of the atom in quest of the seemingly "objective" reality of the electron, we are again brought up short. Werner Heisenberg, one of the pioneers in quantum theory, characterizes reality at that level by denying that atoms or electrons are things:

The electrons which form an atom's shells are no longer things in the sense of classical physics, things which could be unambiguously described by concepts like location, velocity, energy, size. When we get down to the atomic level, the objective world in space and time no longer exists.[12]

From another standpoint, in the Theory of Relativity, Einstein showed that neither space nor time exists apart from the subject's experience of them. They are categories created by our minds for the arrangement of objects and events:

We find that space means nothing apart from our perception of objects, and time means nothing apart from our experience of events. Space begins to appear merely as a fiction created by our own minds, an illegitimate extension to nature of a subjective concept which helps us to understand and describe the arrangement of objects as seen by us; while time appears as a second fiction, serving a similar purpose for the arrangement of events which happen to us. [13]

Sir James Jeans sums up the worldview of modern physics by saying:

We must no longer think of the universe as consisting of solid pieces of matter which persist in time, and move about in space.
    In this way the theory of quanta and the theory of relativity combine forces in leading us to conjecture, with Leibnitz, that matter as ordinarily understood, the matter of solid objects and hard particles, has no existence in reality, and only appears to exist through our observing non-material things in a confused way—through the bias of our human spectacles. [14]

The world as revealed by the modern physics of quantum theory and relativity theory recalls us to our inner spiritual world. At the atomic level the objective world ceases to exist altogether, so that modern physics confronts one ultimately with a vast emptiness outside time and space, but not far removed from the spiritual master's experience of reality as the ultimate perfect emptiness.

If we in fact live in a shadow-world of ultimate emptiness whose objective reality and conflicts are derived from our own psyche, the world is too much with us for a radically spiritual reason. As we are, so is the world because the world derives its fundamental shape and definitions from ourselves, and primarily from our ego, in a way too profound for us to grasp except in the rare case of the spiritual master's experience of reality. As we are, so is the world, in so deep-rooted a sense that the world can and will be transformed only and exactly to the extent that I undergo transformation in myself. What we know "out there" as the most resistant evil reality to be transformed, is in reality "in here" in its primary being.

The precise nature of that correspondence, or identity, between inner and outer worlds is the mystery which Jung was attempting to describe with his theory of Synchronicity, whereby outer events can be increasingly recognized as unifying correlations of a profoundly traveled inner way. Once we begin to see this profound interpenetration of inner and outer worlds in a oneness of reality, the insoluble enigma of the world of evil gives way to the edge of the unifying mystery of Oneness, or of Love, a mystery which we cannot fully understand but which we can in fact move into with our lives and participate in to the extent of experiencing an ever-more-united world in Reality.

It is at this point that there begins to appear the deeper significance of Jesus' teaching that the person who loses self will find it, and of Gandhi's parallel teaching that the satyagrahi must reduce herself to zero. For it is the individual self or ego which goes about defining the world together with its evil and suffering, and it is that ego which then taking itself as a distinct reality confronts its own world of suffering with the demand that it change. Yet the prerequisite for change is, as Jesus points out, in the eye of the beholder. Or as Gandhi teaches, such change becomes possible only when the satyagrahi has so humbled herself that even the very dust could crush her. Only then, and not until then, at the point of being crushed by the dust itself, will the satyagrahi have reduced the ego-self enough to have a living glimpse of Truth, a Truth whose nonviolence can embrace the world. Because until that point of ultimate "I-renunciation" has been reached, the world in its intractable evil will exist in perfect correspondence and identity with the ego, that ego we parade and take for granted yet fail to recognize as the very basis of the world which violates others and is too much with ourselves.

Jesus, we can assume, took something like that ego into the wilderness for 40 days and nights of prayer and fasting, and there underwent an inconceivable night of self-emptying which freed him for the Reality of the kingdom whose dawning he proclaimed when he returned to Galilee. Turn your lives around, he said, for the kingdom of God is at hand—it's right here, open your lives and see. The world in Reality is one. It is one at that depth of self-emptying in love and truth where seeing and being become one, in One, so that the world necessarily reflects the truth of a realized Being. Look, he said to the people in the synagogue, He has sent me to bring good news to the poor, to proclaim freedom to prisoners, to the blind new sight, to set the oppressed free. Look, he said later to the disciples of John, go back and tell John what you've seen and heard: The blind see again, the lame walk, lepers are cleansed, the deaf hear, the dead are raised to life, good news is proclaimed to the poor.

The world around Jesus came alive with unifying signs of the kingdom of oneness he already saw dawning in it. This oneness of inner and outer worlds is also the reason for the striking realism of the parables of the kingdom given by Jesus. Jesus *saw*, in ways no one before him had seen, the presence of the kingdom in the simplest realities of the world. The realism of his parables arises therefore

> from a conviction that there is no mere analogy, but an inward affinity, between the natural order and the spiritual order; or as we might put it in the language of the parables themselves, the Kingdom of God is intrinsically *like* the processes of nature and of the daily life of men. Jesus therefore did not feel the need of making up artificial illustrations for the truths He wished to teach. He found them ready-made by the Maker of man and nature. That human life, including the religious life, is a part of nature is distinctly stated in the well-known passage beginning, "Consider the fowls of the air. . ." (Mt. 6. 26-30; Lk. 12. 24-28).[15]

The events of Jesus' life were a further step-by-step realization of this oneness of inner and outer worlds stated in the realism of the parables. Thus in contradiction to the ritual distinctions and class antagonisms of his society, Jesus welcomed into his community and identified himself with the poor, the oppressed, the disreputable. He became one himself with beggars and lepers, with tax-collectors, with the hungry and thirsty, with the unclothed and strangers, the sick and prisoners, with women, with those who wept and labored, with the lost, the sinners, the separated and rejected ones of the world. He proclaimed good news to these poor: The good news that their rejection and separation in the world is at an end because they are accepted in the One Reality of Love, because whatever surface distinctions may have been imposed, that One is at the center of them and of that world and can be realized in the visible dawning kingdom of oneness signified by Jesus' becoming one with each of them—so that whatever you do to the least of these, you in reality do to me.[16] The kingdom of God is at hand, right here. The world in Reality is one, see it in and through that One Who Loves. The world that Jesus confronted and lived in, reflected naturally and necessarily the

Reality of Oneness which Jesus had emptied himself into so totally in the wilderness. The occasional flashes of oneness of inner and outer worlds in every life which Jung described as Synchronicity took the further form in Jesus' life, because of its "ultimate perfect emptiness," of a beginning-to-be-realized kingdom of God. According to John's Gospel, Jesus in simultaneously seeing and realizing that kingdom in action was establishing a way of living faith for others to follow, and to follow to a point of transformation in the world beyond anything even he himself had done: "I tell you most solemnly, whoever believes in me will perform the same works as I do myself, he will perform even greater works, because I am going to the Father." (John 14.12) Jesus' going to the Father is a further opening of (and invitation to follow) the graceful way into the kingdom, the way of the cross.

Always at the center of the kingdom of Reality which Jesus proclaimed as good news to the poor and saw coming into being, always at the center of the inner and outer kingdom's dawning signs of oneness in the world, was the one sign which gave birth to all the others, the sign of the cross. The cross is the ultimate statement in community of the truth discovered in the wilderness: That complete emptying is complete oneness, that perfect death is perfect life, and that in and through that death and emptying into a night beyond night, then at the zero point, the kingdom of Reality is at hand. The cross gives birth to the kingdom, the kingdom of a new people in a new world. Or more to the point, the cross is that ultimate self-emptying which is our only way into the kingdom, into that transformed world of oneness which is already at hand, just under the iron grasp of the ego.

The cross of suffering love and service to others is the communal fulfillment of oneness in the wilderness. The cross is that loss of self where the unity of inner and outer worlds, which flashed into identity in the wilderness, gets lived and suffered into a complete and total oneness. In our own time of mass suffering, Gandhi has witnessed to the truth of the cross that the world of pain invites our identification with it, and that God or Enlightenment must be found more and more directly in the midst of a suffering people rather than in a Himalayan cave. At the same time, Gandhi's witness in and to the people had as its basis the same radical vision of reality as the Tibetan rimpoches had in their caves: That the external world and the ultimate Self, that unconscious divine Self below the illusions of the ego, are in reality one. And for that reason, the prospect of the world's nonviolent transformation could be understood by him as the embodiment of a perfect act of Self-realization, that single silent thought which Gandhi said could envelop the whole world but had been expressed by no one.

But the emptying-unifying experience of the wilderness and the cross gives birth, as Jesus showed, to the dawning kingdom of a community, and Gandhi's great insight together with the movement he founded was weakest in its emphasis—parallel to that of the rimpoches— on the unifying power of the single individual, which in the satyagraha movement tended in practice to leave it up to Gandhi himself. The point is not that one person cannot become so crushed by the dust as to realize the single silent thought Gandhi spoke of, but that the ego plays profound tricks even under the dust. A communal process helps to expose them. A community of satyagrahis embracing the darkness of the cross together is a more direct way to global oneness than the thought of any single guru. In the nonviolent community of the future, each member should feel equally the invitation and responsibility to help her sisters, brothers, and herself deepen in a mutual discipline of getting lost in the ultimate perfect emptiness from which a transformed world can emerge. For the way into that ultimate emptiness, and into a unified world of persons which is its other side, requires a oneness in Love so deep that each will accept and become the innermost Reality of the other.

1Pyarelal, Mahatma Gandhi: *The Last Phase, Volume II* (Ahmedabad, Navajivan Publishing House: 1958), pp. 808-9.

2*ibid.*, p. 781.

3*ibid.*, p. 784.

4'C.G. Jung, *Memories, Dreams, Reflections* (Vintage: 1963), pp. 137-8.

5On Jung and Einstein, see Ira Progoff, *Jung, Synchronicity, and Human Destiny* (Julian Press: 1973), pp. 147-58. Jung's most complete statement of Synchronicity is his essay, "Synchronicity: An Acausal Connecting Principle," in *The Structure and Dynamics of the Psyche,* Vol. 8 of *The Collected Works* (Princeton University Press: 1969), pp. 417-531. There are numerous references to Synchronicity and discussions of its meaning in C.G. Jung, *Letters, Vol. I: 1906-1950* (Princeton University Press: 1973), ed. Gerhard Adler & Aniela Jaffe.

6Progoff, pp. 29, 108-16.

7*The Asian Journal of Thomas Merton*, edited from his original notebooks by Naomi Burton, Brother Patrick Hart & James Laughlin (New Directions: 1973), p. 143.

8*loc. sit.*

9*The Teachings of Ramana Maharshi*, edited by Arthur Osborne (Samuel Weiser: 1971), p. 86.

10Thomas Merton, "Is 'the World' a Problem?", *Katallagete* (Spring 1974), p. 32.

11See Arthur Eddington's famous "parable of the two writing desks" in his introduction to *The Nature of the Physical World* (Cambridge: 1928) in which he shows the shadow-world in which we actually live.

12Werner Heisenberg, *Der Teil und das Ganze* (Munchen: 1969), pp. 63-4. Quoted by Arthur Koestler, *The Roots of Coincidence* (Vintage: 1972), p. 51.

13Sir James Jeans, *The New Background of Science* (Cambridge: 1934), pp. 99-100.

14*ibid.*, pp. 294-5.

15C.H.Dodd, *The Parables of the Kingdom* (James Nisbet & Co.: 1958), pp. 21-22.

16Norman Perrin is typical of New Testament scholars in declaring: "Of all the descriptive titles that have been applied to Jesus through the centuries, the one that sums up his historical appearance best is the one whose currency owes so much to Bultmann: 'Jesus is the Proclaimer of the Kingdom of God.'" Norman Perrin, *Rediscovering the Teaching of Jesus* (Harper & Row: 1967), p. 54. Joachim Jeremias characterizes Jesus' proclamation of the kingdom as "the present dawning of the transfiguration of the world." But the kingdom's most decisive feature, he says, is Jesus' proclaiming it as good news to "the poor"—to the oppressed and disreputable, and in Jesus' wider sense of "the poor," to all those who experienced pain and rejection. Joachim Jeremias, *New Testament Theology: The Proclamation of Jesus* (Charles Scribner's Sons:1971), pp.108-13.

4
Stopping the World in an End-Time

In the Fall of 1974, a small event took place which so symbolized the mood of our time that it was reported and editorialized on in newspapers across the world: *The Bulletin of Atomic Scientists*, a periodical begun after World War II by scientists anxious to avert a nuclear holocaust, moved the hands on its symbolic doomsday clock three minutes closer to midnight—to nine minutes to twelve. The *Bulletin*'s message corresponded to the world's sense of its own time. A sense of ultimate violence was already abroad, and the doomsday clock only confirmed it. Due to a host of historical factors—global famine, injustice, and terrorism; failure of the Strategic Arms Limitation Talks, continued development of nuclear weapons systems, India's first atomic test, Britain's renewal of testing, worldwide proliferation of nuclear technology—and most of all, due to a pervasive sense of inevitable, deepening violence at the heart of our human spirit in the nuclear age, people everywhere could recognize the truth that we have only a few minutes left. In our own time, because of specific historical causes, we are living at the end of time.

But why the failure of Christian thought to recognize and come to terms with our end-time? Why have Christian theologians in particular not been able to recognize that history has caught up with the ultimate human crisis envisioned by the Jesus of the Gospels, the crisis of a sinfully deserved end-time? Why is the historical confirmation of Jesus' apocalyptic vision, a vision once an embarrassment to modernized Christians but now borne out amply by their reality, so absent from the thought of those whose scriptures warn them to be alert and responsive to an end-time?

Apart from the sectarian doctrines of Jehovah's Witnesses and others and a few prophetic voices like William Stringfellow's, there is virtual silence among Christians concerning a doomsday truth which the world has already recognized in itself, and which the church once knew well in the context of its good news. Evidence of this silence can be found in the dominant political theology since the beginning of the nuclear age, "Christian realism," as developed by Reinhold Niebuhr and his followers. Christian realism has repressed the central reality of our end-time: the imminent destruction of all life on earth. It is a theology which has emphasized the reality of sin in history but has never faced squarely the emerging end of history through sin. Christian realism has continued to say that however critical war, and nuclear war in particular, is to our time, its significance should not be seen as terminal—or more to the point, need not make nonviolence a human imperative.

But historical oversight ("seeing over" a major element of our own history) is equally present in the more recent thought of liberation theology, which in giving expression to that other human imperative of our end-time, the need for liberation from oppression, is so deep in insight. Liberation theology confronts profoundly suffering humanity's need for freedom, yet forgets in its analysis and vision the simultaneous human need for a spreading global peace, and thus for means of struggle consistent with that end. It is not that liberation theology espouses violence, as its critics often misrepresent it. It is simply that liberation theology seldom speaks to the human, ethical need today to *resist* the means of war as well as the means of oppression.[1] That freedom's side of our twofold moral imperative should be emphasized by those theologians who speak out of a history of oppression is understandable and right. But that the ethical imperative of peaceful means is ignored as the clock ticks toward midnight is as unfortunate for oppressed peoples, meant to inherit the earth, as it is for those who now rape and exploit the earth and prepare its end. We have only a few minutes left, for oppressed as well as oppressors.

This criticism of Christian theologies, in terms of their bypassing one side of the dominant violence of our time and the moving hands on the clock, gives way to a question: Is there in fact—or in a faithful vision of reality—a way to unite the two moral-political imperatives of our end-time, liberation and peace? A first purpose here is simply to underscore the crucial importance of the problem, that of finding a way to both liberation and peace. The point is that we are blind to the full historical dimensions of humanity's current suffering (forms of oppression and war intertwined), and can make no response to the more terrible prospect in store, if we fail to take account of the need for such a union. The winning of liberation demands history for its struggle, and history demands nonviolence. Nonviolent liberation is the ethic of an end-time.

But again the question: How to envision nonviolent liberation in terms of the overwhelming realities of our end-time, from global exploitation and famine to poised nuclear missiles? And silence descends. Our spirit goes dead. It cannot see the way, and therefore ceases to hear the question. Our spirit is so full of the death of our time that we cannot even begin to see a liberating way through that time, the way to an integral freedom and peace, to a transformed world. Which is, I believe, the explanation for Christian thought's failure to hear the question, or to remember Jesus' warning to watch and wait.

We lack the roots necessary for a response. In the West in particular, we have lost any sense of a spirituality with a radical enough critique of reality to sustain a theology of revolutionary transformation. Judaeo-Christian contemplatives have offered such a critique but it has remained too much a part of a tradition which has insisted dogmatically on the reality of the individual self. Because the individual self has always been accepted as real by even the church, reality in Western eyes and hearts and societies is "set," set without any inner restraint on a world of technological fantasies; set in a direction of historically inexorable violence, out of which our nuclear end-time is the logical spiritual conclusion.

As contemplative traditions have insisted with unanimity, the individual self imposes a vision of separation and brokenness upon a world which in Reality is one. Western societies have not only accepted without question the individual self and its fantasies, but have celebrated and consumerized them with vengeance. The result is our nuclear end-time.

One of the most profound indictments of the West's self-imposed commitment to ultimate violence is the work of Dostoevsky, though that work's literally self-indicting nature is not often acknowledged, and the logical spiritual imperative of a complete self-emptying hardly ever drawn from it. Dostoevsky shows that the nature of the world of the self in Western consciousness is one of willful violence. The basic psychological law of the world of the self which Dostoevsky experienced and portrayed was the circle of hurt-and-be-hurt, based on the realities of self-awareness and the will's subsequent involvement in power:"What the will wants more than anything else is awareness of itself, and it will subvert every motive to gain this satisfaction."[2] The spiritually radical truth of this analysis holds good for every form of will to power and violence from superpower bargaining positions to the obviously necessary self-assertions of our private lives. All ways of upholding the world of the self derive from the same willful source within and point to ultimate violence and destruction.

The way to reverse the movements of a self-destructive world was taught by Dostoevsky's monk Zossima in *The Brothers Karamazov*:

> For Zossima—and for Dostoevsky—there can only be one answer: a total acceptance of others, all others. There is only one right way to accept (the wrong ways are endless), and that is to humble oneself before all others; and there is only one way to humble oneself (the wrong ways are endless), and that is to see oneself as endlessly and hopelessly more sinful than all others. At the first impulse to see oneself as less sinful than anyone, the will and the self spring to birth, bringing with them separation, hardness, and the endless duels of Dostoevsky's world.[3]

The discipline of a constantly experienced sense of one's own radical sin and emptiness, as the basis for a self-giving love, was Dostoevsky's way out of the West's circular violence of the self. His primary resource for that understanding, as shown in *The Legend of the Grand Inquisitor*, was Jesus' rejection of his temptations to power and his self-emptying experience in the wilderness.

In a Mid-East society 19 centuries before the atomic bomb, Jesus could see and feel a pattern of self-founded violence developing in the world because he first experienced it himself in the wilderness. He came out of that self-confronting and self-emptying experience in the wilderness to proclaim the truth of the kingdom in an imminent end-time, a truth of the kingdom conveyed in the Gospels with Jesus' emphasis on *metanoia* as the only way into it. Today *metanoia* (which "repentance" fails to express) is the still-seldom-explored way into Jesus' life and kingdom of Reality. It is that *metanoia* change of heart and soul, through an inconceivably radical renunciation of self, which is the truth of the wilderness and the continuing way into nonviolent liberation and a transformed world. Now as then, *metanoia* can begin to become possible in the midst of the world's (our own) violence and untruth through a kind of wilderness retreat: along such wilderness paths in our own time as the life and work of Thomas Merton, or the disciplines of Zen and Tibetan Buddhism, or most recently through a way worked out in a native American wilderness, the way of "the warrior" as taught by the Yaqui Indian Don Juan in Carlos Castaneda's books. This last and most recent expression of the self-emptying way of *metanoia* is helpful to consider, in relation to our failure to envision the way of non-violent liberation, because Don Juan identifies precisely in his apprentice Castaneda as in all of us the fundamental obstacle to a new and transformed world, the iron hold our self has on the old, violent world.

The point is made most explicit by Don Juan near the conclusion of *Tales of Power*: The reason for our blindness to Reality, and to the kingdom of a new world present in it, is that the world we think we see is only a view, a description of the world. As Don Juan says, "We are complacently caught in our particular view of the world, which compels us to feel and act as if we knew everything about the world."[4] The purpose of a teacher toward an apprentice lies therefore in stopping his or her view of the world—"stopping the internal dialogue," or simply "stopping the world," as the self-emptying experience of illumination is described at different points in the apprentice's spiritual journey. In order to see the totality of oneself, a kingdom of Reality which is neither within nor without, where self and world are instead one, one must stop the world as it is known—which is the world of the ego-self knowing it, a self-defined world of violence and spiritual impotence. The world is stopped as the self is reduced to zero. The world we think we see is merely a view, and the view a reflection of an ego. What matters is to travel into the totality of Reality, an ever-deepening journey into the kingdom which becomes possible only after we have stopped the reality of our own ego-bound world.

"Stopping the world of violence" does not mean that violence would thereby cease to exist in the world. Mass starvation and arms races would still be there. Nor does stopping the world mean that a spiritual aspirant would become so absorbed in a mystical experience that s(he) would no longer care about or respond to the suffering and violence in our human family (which is not mysticism but a pseudo-spiritual cynicism, a common sign of death in our end-time). Stopping the world, through a self-emptying way of *metanoia*, is neither global magic nor individual hypocrisy. It is simply an opening—an opening "in the wilderness" to the truth and vision that the kingdom of Reality is at hand, a radically indispensable opening if that kingdom is to be realized. The kingdom of a new world is at hand, to the extent that we can make that endless journey into the overwhelming Reality never seen before the *metanoia* reversal of our hearts and minds and vision. The kingdom is the world in Reality. In the struggle for nonviolent liberation, anything is possible because God is Real.

My home is in a valley in British Columbia whose beauty sometimes makes me feel that to find the Reality which transforms and unites, one need only walk up the side of a mountain at dawn, sit under a pine tree, and watch the sunlight glide slowly into the valley like yellow wings. But that translucent Reality of oneness is a long way from the self-emptying darkness of *metanoia*, a falling through one's own night spaces where the ego's grasps at reality are frantic and futile. In a sense no one can choose *metanoia*. One can only choose *metanoia*'s situation of powerlessness, a point in one's life whereby one is exposed simply and nakedly to *metanoia*'s ruthless destruction of self-images; as Tibetan monks have chosen the Himalayan cave in the hope that self-defenses against Reality would be minimized—but not always the case, and especially not the case when their resources were such as to carve a new and more shining reality of self out of rock and silence. Then a more likely exposure to *metanoia* would come in the wilderness of New Delhi or New York, finding the wilderness by facing the truth—through human exposure to one's friends, lover, children, self in solitude. Prepare to stop the world of the self by first discovering where and how the self is most vulnerable to the truth. Choose to live through that *metanoia* situation in truth, and in spite of one's self, the world stops.

In its essence, then, the *metanoia* situation is one of poverty—a poverty which in our end-time of mass starvation and weapons systems needs to take the radical, double form of spiritual *and* material poverty as a single living truth, where inner and outer liberation are one, a living poverty which is neither within nor without but rather total in its naked acceptance of Reality. The kingdom of Reality is at hand, but once again—in our end-time, as in Jesus' sense of the end—the kingdom is accessible only through the wilderness and its culmination in a nonviolent cross (of violence suffered in love) which remains a sign of contradiction, and a continuing way to resist and stop the world of violence.

This truth that we must somehow stop or reverse the only world we know (by reversing our lives), while fundamental to entry into the kingdom proclaimed in the Gospels, is strange to Western ears accustomed to reducing the sense of *metanoia* to repentance. But the need to stop the world we know was familiar to the best-known practitioner of nonviolent liberation since Jesus of Nazareth, Mohandas Gandhi. Gandhi in fact founded his philosophy of nonviolent liberation, the philosophy of *satyagraha* or "truth-force," on the disciplines of just such a teaching as it is expressed in the classic Hindu texts of the *Bhagavad-Gita*, the *Isha Upanishad*, and Patanjali's *Yoga Sutras*. In the *Yoga Sutras* the point is made by saying that when a person becomes so at one with Reality as to be constant in his or her *ahimsa*, or loving nonviolence; then all living creatures will cease to feel enmity and violence in that person's presence—an even more radical stopping of the world of violence than the initial opening of *metanoia*. This is not only *metanoia* but a fulfillment of the wilderness experience in a person's life and community, a presence of the kingdom which Gandhi sought all his life in his very concrete experiments in truth.

The difference between Gandhi, however, and the traditional teacher of contemplative disciplines, such as Don Juan, is that Gandhi made a wilderness discipline, or one normally practiced in solitude, the very basis of a community whose purpose was to live a revolution in every aspect of social and political life. Stopping the world of personal violence, and stopping the world of social violence, were seen as one way, a way based on a radical contemplative discipline. As Raghavan Iyer remarks in his *Moral and Political Thought of Mahatma Gandhi*: "As early as 1903 Gandhi studied Patanjali's *Yoga Sutra*. No Indian before him had made this book the basis of the ethical discipline of people engaged in politics and social work as Gandhi did in the Satyagrahashram at Sabarmati."[5]

It can be suggested that it is just such a radically disciplined *metanoia*, in which the contemplative life is the constant inward dimension of a struggle for justice, that is the key to opening up the otherwise impossible way of nonviolent liberation in our end-time.

The lack of a radical inward dimension of struggle is the explanation not only of our present inability to confront a doomsday reality but also of the unfulfilled nonviolence of the past ("the nonviolence of the 60's") so often cited as rationale for our unwillingness to engage the truth of nonviolence at a deeper level. But for there to come into being a genuine way of nonviolent liberation, deep enough in Reality to transform our end-time into a new beginning, communities seeking that way will need to take a careful, critical view of the history of nonviolent movements, especially Gandhi's and King's.

In the case of Dr. King, he has been the subject of only one thorough biography, Stephen B. Oates's *Let The Trumpet Sound,* a helpful book in filling in gaps of personal history and in understanding the events around King's life but still lacking a sense of the inner person. Because Martin Luther King more than any other person showed the way of nonviolence to Americans (and much of the world), he needs to be understood and loved more critically than he has been by nonviolent communities seeking a way of liberation, and ultimate transformation in our age. Special attention needs to be given to the question of how fully King met the radical demands of *metanoia* in himself, and to what extent he demonstrated those demands to a wider community.[6]

The same need for critical attention is true of Gandhi, particularly from a feminist standpoint. Gandhi often spoke of the injustice against women yet failed at important points to respond to it adequately in either a social or personal sense. (Witness not only his honest admissions of violating Kasturbai Gandhi early in their marriage, but also the moral tyranny of his later efforts to steer her course.) At the same time, Gandhi's liberation ethic of experimenting in truth was profoundly different from and resistant to the male ideologies and means of both capitalist and Marxist worlds.

The nonviolent liberation necessary in our end-time lies in the exact-opposite direction of any piety whereby we venerate the images of others or (less obviously but more profoundly) ourselves for the sake of staying where we are. *Metanoia* empties one of all such images and idolatry.

The biblical witness to an end-time, given especially in the Book of Revelation, is that one lives out the ultimate freedom, in an ultimate crisis, through a faithful way of resistance and contemplation: resistance to a reign of death, and contemplation of a coming Reality of Christ whose final meaning is the new Jerusalem, in a new heaven and a new earth. An end-time is fulfilled in the second coming of Christ. But what is the nature of that second coming?

William Stringfellow writes on this point:

> The excited imagery in Revelation of the Second Coming of the Lord, with midair apparitions and other marvels, may have caused some to dwell upon the texts literalistically—to fix upon

the wonders rather than upon the excitement of hope. But we can be saved from so demeaning the Second Coming of Christ if we see that, for all its mystery, the Second Advent is faithful to the mission of the First Advent, and is no disjuncture or disruption. [7]

The First Advent involved a continuous self-emptying poverty in the life of Jesus of Nazareth and those around him: the birth of a child in a cave, an obscure period of growth in village and desert, the *metanoia* of a wilderness retreat, and a public life of poverty, compassion, and resistance in truth; finally, execution as criminal and a resurrected life in the midst of a despairing community—whose lives then took on again the life of Jesus, in a self-emptying poverty of love and truth for others.

If (as I believe Stringfellow is right in saying) the mysterious second coming of Christ is faithful to the meaning of the first, is no disjuncture or disruption of a history in which Christ is already present, yet is a consummation of all that can be hoped for from Jesus' life, death, and resurrection, then the Reality of Christ will be known again only in and through a self-emptying poverty, a *metanoia*-based force of truth and love, capable in a final crisis of liberating and transforming it into the community of a new Jerusalem, in a new heaven and a new earth.

The most fruitful question raised by the early Christian faith in a second coming is not one of objective identity—what external form that Reconciling Reality of Christ might take in a final crisis, and precisely when—but rather the more pointed question in ourselves of how a community might now live in most complete fidelity to the way of truth and love given in the first coming, and thus welcome most profoundly in ourselves the Reality found through that living, self-emptying poverty which is the process of non-violent transformation.

The way of *metanoia*, a way of stopping the world in an end-time of global violence is, above all, a way not of speculation but of practice—a way of living and acting out a day-to-day personal and communal struggle for a liberating, transforming truth for humanity, after the example of Gandhi in his experiments in truth and according to the good news of Jesus that the truth is at the same time the life and the way, a nonviolent way of the cross. The way to stop the world of violence—by realizing the kingdom of Reality already present beneath it— the way to witness and experience that Reality transforming the world into a oneness of love which is our only real freedom, is for us to experiment in each of our lives, and in community, in a more radically emptying truth of nonviolence than the self will admit is possible.

My world over the ten years, 1966-75, was really two worlds, a world of resistance and a world of contemplation. The two worlds existed on opposite sides of a border, dividing the United States and Canada, the two countries in which I am a citizen.

On the U.S. side of the border, my life was one of resistance—resistance to the war in Indochina, to the global policies the war expressed, and to a deeper spirit of death in America. This world of resistance to killing was experienced mainly in Honolulu, Hawaii, as a member of two resistance communities: in the late 60's, the Hawaii Resistance; in the early 70's, catholic Action of Hawaii, a local chapter of the War Resisters League.

The other world I knew, on the Canadian side of the border, was a world of contemplation. I have always returned to my original home in Canada in order to write—or more exactly, to work through questions of evil, violence, and nonviolence which have opened to truth only through a sustained period of struggle, and of writing through the stages of the struggle. This world of contemplation has been my home in Hedley, British Columbia, a town of 500 people living between towering red-tainted rock bluffs at the entrance to a canyon, where Twenty Mile Creek curves out of the mountains' shadows and flows into the Similkameen River.

Since 1973, when Shelley, our children, and I returned from Honolulu to B.C., the world of contemplation in Hedley has involved a particular struggle related to the world of resistance. The more reflective side of that struggle, in the effort to write this book, has been the question of humanity's nonviolent transformation in our end-time, when there is little time left for the radical changes needed in spirit and society for the world to be preserved. But beneath the end-time question, and also related to the world of resistance, has been a more personal struggle within Shelley's and my marriage.

Our resistance experience in Hawaii taught us different truths. In my case, it was the truth, learned through our catholic Action campaign at Pacific Air Force Headquarters, that anything is possible through the work of a tiny community of resisters responding with truth to overwhelming power. In Shelley's case, that was a part of the truth, for she had lived through the same resistance campaign with its extraordinary success in penetrating Air Force security, focusing Hawaii's attention on the bombing being targetted from Hickam Air Base, and forcing the Government to withdraw all the felony charges in our trial. But another side of the truth of Hawaii for Shelley was the fact that within that campaign, and specifically from me, she had experienced the same sexist attitudes which she was resisting in the society as a whole. Resistance in Hawaii had meant the experience of being violated in our marriage as well as the experience of overcoming the U.S. Government. And for that reason, as we began in Hedley to envision our future return from B.C. to the States, we experienced a deepening split—between my belief that my work should once again be with the resistance community in Honolulu, and Shelley's commitment to a wholeness of nonviolence which she had not experienced there and thought could be better found elsewhere. We both felt strong personal reasons for working on opposite sides of the ocean.

The process of struggling in Hedley with the question of an inconceivable nonviolent transformation in humanity was linked to the deepening struggle in our marriage, with the outcome in each case becoming more and more of an impasse. How could one even begin to envision the possibility of a transformation of humanity when reconciliation seemed impossible with the person I loved most? Our conflict, centered on the Hickam blood-pouring action, seemed to involve the deepest values of each of us. Shelley thought the action was wrong in taking place, if it involved my unilaterally cancelling an earlier agreement with her, as she had in fact felt the night before the action took place. I thought our agreement had been something else, and that it was wrong to suspend, or afterwards regret because of a misunderstanding, the action which broke open the whole campaign and raised the public's awareness of the war.

From the same conflict over the Hickam action, a more immediate concern than the question of our return to the States was the key importance the event had assumed, as a paradigm, in the question I was pursuing in the book. The Hickam blood-pouring and what followed from it seemed to me to be symbols of a deeper and wider possibility. But if the paradigmatic experience was valid for only one of two of the people most intimately involved in it, of what use was it as a reflective base for a wider community? On that level, the struggle took the form of a widening split between the worlds of resistance and contemplation: Because Shelley and I disagreed on our understanding of the Hawaii experience, it was impossible to absorb its truth fully into the contemplative world of Hedley, as was done before in the writing of books based on a resistance experience. After Shelley moved to Vancouver School of Theology for her studies for the ministry and I remained in Hedley to work on the book, I continued to come up against this block between us in the form it had taken in my own consciousness, a block between resistance experience and a way forward in reflection. The two realities of resistance and contemplation stood divided and facing one another, like the great bluffs at the entrance to Twenty Mile Canyon, two opposed and irreconcilable rocks. I spent days walking up the road alongside the creek and meditating between those rock bluffs, without the realities in my world ever showing any more signs of coming together than the bluffs did.

After months of this impasse in Hedley, when the ratio of thinking to actual writing had become about a thousand to one, I came very close to giving up on the book—and despairing of our marriage as well, in a very concrete sense, for to give up on the book would have meant to return to the only other work of value I could conceive of for my future, working with the resistance community in Hawaii without ever having reconciled with Shelley the questions raised there. (We continued to go over these questions together but had reached a state of near exhaustion at ever finding a common understanding.) Moreover, to return to resistance after having despaired of integrating it into a deeper way of transformation would be to choose a way without hope. There was no truthful way out of the struggle which had taken over my world, yet that world had become so confining in spirit that the temptation to simply thrash my way out of it was almost overwhelming. Until finally a force gathered one day out of the violence of the Similkameen Valley and stopped the world of my violence. It happened on Hedley's May Day.

May Day in Hedley is unlike the international labor holiday. Its purpose, in a small town with many children, is simply to celebrate the spring festival in a way that will give our children the most fun. There is a big parade—floats, horses, kids in costume down the main street—with half of Hedley in the parade and the other half along the dirt sidewalks applauding. Prizes are given to kids for costumes, pets, floats, bike decorations, and just being there. After the parade and prizes are a Maypole dance, races, a tug of war between the men and the women, a ballgame in which everyone who wants to plays, and a dance at night free for everyone under 15.

In the Spring of 1974, I inadvertently became chairperson of the Hedley May Day Committee, at a public meeting when all the other nominees had declined the office. The diversion from my writing and research came as a relief, an opportunity to serve a more visible community than future readers of an unwriteable book. Our Committee worked hard in preparing for May Day but we discovered early on the morning it arrived that our preparations were inadequate: Rain was falling sporadically, and the crepe-paper floats in garages were not water-proof. It was while I was panicking over the weather prospects that I received a call from Fred, who is known by some of the kids in town as "the pigeon-man" because Fred raises homing pigeons and other birds—which had included geese, until late one night some unidentified persons raided the house where the geese slept and shot them all. It was not an unheard-of event in Hedley, where teen-agers especially get bored and seek excitement. Fred had offered a $100 reward for information but there were no takers.

On the phone, in his thick accent which I could never understand well, Fred was asking me something about his entering a late float in the parade. I said sure and went back to worrying over the rain.

An hour later, when the weather had cleared enough for the parade to be ready to begin, I was walking along the line of floats admiring them when I came to a quiet circle of people near the end. They were looking at Fred's late entry. The float was his motor-cart. (Fred is disabled and drives a little motor-cart around town.) The motor-cart had a large sign on the back of it, with the thawing body of a dead goose stuck in the middle of the sign. The sign, written in blood, read: "The parents of the children who did this should be shot, too." Fred was sitting on the cart grinning, not maliciously but with genuine pleasure. He asked me how I liked his float.

After some silence, I said there was another owner of birds in Hedley, whose chickens had been raided and killed. But she had helped the children with their own floats for the parade.

Fred smiled and said his was a really good float. It should be in the parade.

As I was standing there anticipating the reaction of Hedley to Fred's float and wondering what I could do to persuade him to take it away, an older friend and parade official came up to us. He smiled and told Fred he could now move his float into position for the parade. Fred nodded happily. The parade began.

When the parade was over, one of the best in Hedley's history of May Days, I came across Fred still smiling and puttering his dead-goose float around. He said he'd had some good talks with people along the way about his float. Then he looked at me closely and added: "I know you didn't want my float, Jim, but you were wrong. You can't keep the world out of the parade."

The dance that night at the Community Hall, which I watched from the refreshment booth, was like being hit again and again with the shock of cold ecstasy felt in summer in diving into a deep pool in the creek: the free beauty of the children, all of whom came to the dance, from ages four or five on up; the genuine country rhythm of Irving and Ila Nelson on their steel guitar and drums, the owners of a small ranch who herd cows when they're not (usually not) playing music at dances; the joy of young and old people dancing wildly who "don't know how to dance" (hardly anyone in Hedley does) but still dance until they drop, like burnt-out candles, into the slat-backed chairs on the side.

After the dance, a strange depth of happiness made it difficult to sleep. When I got up early the next morning and unfolded the newspaper at the door, I learned from the headlines what had taken place elsewhere in the world on the same day in which Hedley was enjoying the beauty of May Day in the Similkameen Valley: India had exploded its first atomic bomb. The biggest terror bombing in the history of Ireland had shaken the streets of Dublin. An army of American police had shot it out with the SLA in Los Angeles, while crowds watched and cheered. Hedley May Day, May 18, 1974.

You can't keep the world out of the parade.

A different kind of cold shock hit then, but not horror at the world either. A new sense of Fred's words: You can't keep the world out of the parade. If one could only absorb and live deeply enough the full reality of Hedley in the Similkameen Valley, then the world in its fullest beauty and pain, in its depth of good and evil, neither cancelling the other, would come home to life in Hedley (or whatever unlikely place for enlightenment from the world). The worlds of resistance and contemplation would be one, just as the two sides of Shelley's and my experience of Hawaii were in fact one reality, just as there was a depth of good and evil in the Hickam action to be fully acknowledged on both sides. You can't keep the world out of the parade.

It took a few more months to live through that understanding to the point where I could act on it. Then one day I sat down and wrote, more quickly and easily than I had ever written anything before, the first chapter of this book. It said in effect that you (meaning I) can't keep the full truth out of the Hickam action, any more than you can keep the world out of the parade. Shelley was right in holding on to her feminist truth and criticism of the resistance experience, whose acknowledgment finally from my side was truth enough for a way of hope, however imperfect it made an action and campaign which were in any case only the small signs of a beginning, not the ends I had made them. Hedley's May Day, and Fred with his dead-goose float, had stopped the world I thought I knew—had broken it open to a world I'd never known, in Hedley or anywhere else. The world of violence, of irreconcilable realities, got stopped in my case by a symbol as accurate as it was unchosen by the world and self it represented: That poor dead goose came as one person's way of *metanoia*.

The kingdom is the world in Reality, a Reality experienced then in Shelley's and my marriage at a depth of oneness unknown since we first came together. And in another shock of Reality (which C.G. Jung would call "Synchronicity"), a friend who came to visit us in Hedley pointed out on a map spread out on our kitchen table that the most destructive weapons system in history, the U.S. Trident submarine, was in the beginning process of being based just south of our B.C./Washington State border, a short space from Hedley on the road map. One didn't have to go to Hawaii to resist. The world had come home to Twenty Mile Creek. The nuclear world was becoming one with the world of contemplation, and in so doing offered the further integrating possibility of a transnational resistance movement, the resistance to a borderline doomsday base of Canadians and Americans together, in a way that hadn't happened before. The world of oneness is found through a more radically emptying truth of nonviolence than the self will admit is possible.

You can't keep the world out of the parade, and the parade in absorbing the world keeps on going, keeps on dancing—through the outer crust of the world's violence into the kingdom of oneness at its core.

1This is true, for example, in the theologies of liberation of Juan Luis Segundo and Gustavo Gutierrez.

In Volume III of his important five-volume work, *A Theology for Artisans of a New Humanity* (Orbis Books: 1974), Segundo addresses briefly the question, "Was God 'nonviolent'?" (pp. 163-69). His answer is that Jesus as God incarnate was necessarily involved in violence: 1) because in the human situation there is no concrete love without violence; 2) because "in any process of evangelization there is necessarily a good dose of violence" (the evangelical signs of Jesus' cures were violent by overwhelming their recipients' power to choose the kingdom on their own); 3) because Jesus as human necessarily loved first those closest to him (thus showing a violence of discrimination), judged people *en masse*, and used physical violence on the merchants in the temple—all forms of violence deriving from the human limitations of time and Jesus' needs in getting across his message in the short term given him.

This discussion by Segundo may serve the purpose of a response to the imperialistic assumptions and legalistic views of "nonviolence" which govern most questions of violence and nonviolence addressed to liberation theologians. But it is inadequate as a response to the real question of means which is crucial to a theology of freeing people from oppressive structures, especially in an age of ultimate violence.

Gustavo Gutierrez in his *Theology of Liberation* (Orbis Books: 1973) makes even less explicit mention of the question of violence, suggesting its moral dilemma most sharply in his discussion of class struggle: "In the context of class struggle today, to love one's enemies presupposes recognizing and accepting that one has class enemies and that it is necessary to combat them. It is not a question of having no enemies, but rather of not excluding them from our love. But love does not mean that the oppressors are no longer enemies, nor does it eliminate the radicalness of the combat against them. 'Love of enemies' does not ease tensions; rather it challenges the whole system and becomes a subversive formula." (p. 276)

Segundo and Gutierrez are characteristic of Latin American theologians of liberation in giving no sign of being familiar with the nonviolent liberation theologies, based on practice, of Mohandas Gandhi and Martin Luther King, whose whole purpose was "love of enemies while challenging the whole system."

2 Edward Wasiolek, *Dostoevsky: The Major Fiction* (M.I.T. Press: 1964), p. 55.

3 *ibid.*, p. 177.

4 Carlos Castaneda, *Tales of Power* (Simon and Schuster: 1974), p. 231.

5 Ragnavan Iyer, *The Moral and Political Thought of Mahatma Gandhi* (Oxford University Press: 1973), p. 9.

6 See Julius Lester's harsh but loving critique of King in the Winter '74 *Katallagete*.

7 William Stringfellow, *An Ethic for Christians and Other Aliens in a Strange Land* (Word Books: 1973), p. 153.

5
Invitation

In Jesus' discourse on the end of the world, it is said: "And with the increase of lawlessness, love in most people will grow cold; but the person who stands firm to the end will be freed." (Matthew 24:12-13)

BANGOR, Washington—A tiny room here with dozens of dials and glowing screens pitches, rolls and simulates the lurching, sickening movement of a submarine in trouble.

On the waterfront, a mammoth hole is being pumped dry and dug deep into the bottom of Hood Canal to make room for one of history's most awesome weapons.

The emergence of the Trident submarine base here is accelerating.

Yesterday, 146 members of the Puget Sound Chambers of Commerce took their annual tour through the 7,700-acre base that will be home port for 10 of the huge, missile-firing "supersubs."

Now about 30 per cent complete, it gleams with new fixtures and structures reflecting the latest in architectural and engineering design. . .

The townhouses and dormitory-like buildings where the Trident men will live resemble large, expensive condominiums. Windows look out on the snow-capped Olympics. Colorful playgrounds nestle among clusters of frame houses. . .

It is all in one of the most beautiful of Hood Canal settings. The Olympics and fir-covered hills form a dramatic backdrop. And deer, fox and pheasants still roam the woods of the base, Navy officers told the visiting businessmen.

(Seattle Times, July 14, 1978.)

I do not know if deer, fox, and pheasants roamed any woods around the Nazi extermination camps of Auschwitz and Buchenwald, nor if the S.S. quarters there resembled the townhouses of the

73

Trident men. But we do have reports that the visiting businessmen of such companies as I.A. Topf and Sons, who manufactured the furnaces for Nazi genocide, were given tours of their investments in incineration like the tour now provided by the U.S. Navy to the members of the Chamber of Commerce. There are, of course, differences between the Nazis' final solution and our own: Their genocide was of the Jewish race. Ours is of the human race. They carried out genocide under a totalitarian state. We prepare the world's holocaust in freedom. Though both crimes are unimaginable, the extent of our holocaust and the depth of our responsibility for it are greater than the Nazis'. Love in most people will grow cold.

The following interview took place at the end of time. (That time is now.) It was carried by no public media, only the consciousness of a person. The interview began and ended in complete silence.

What is Trident?

Trident is the end of the world.

What do you mean?

Trident is a nuclear submarine being built now which will be able to destroy 408 cities or areas at one time, each with a blast five times more powerful than the Hiroshima bomb. Trident is 2,040 Hiroshimas. One Trident submarine can destroy any country on earth. A fleet of Trident submarines (30 are planned) can end life on earth.

I don't understand.

Good. We're getting somewhere. What is it you don't understand?

A submarine which equals 2,040 Hiroshimas. How can anyone understand that?

Begin with a meditation: To understand Trident say the word "Hiroshima." Reflect on its meaning for one second. Say and understand "Hiroshima" again. And again. And again. 2,040 times . Assuming you're able to understand Hiroshima in one second, you'll be able to understand Trident in 34 minutes. That's one Trident submarine. To understand the destructive power of the whole Trident fleet, it would take you 17 hours, devoting one second to each Hiroshima.

Your meditation is impossible. To understand Hiroshima alone would take a lifetime.

You *do* understand. Hiroshima was the end of our ability to imagine our destructive power, or to measure its consequences. Trident is the end of the world.

How does one live at the end of the world?

By beginning a new one. Stop Trident, stop the world in an end-time, and build a new world.

You've lost me again. Stopping Trident does sound like stopping the world—not a very feasible goal. You've been reading too much of Carlos Castaneda. And the world Don Juan stops is a long way from Trident and the Pentagon.

It's not Don Juan but Gandhi, and Jesus before him, who show the way to turn an end-time into a new beginning.

You mean the power of nonviolence, the power of the cross?

Yes.

What about the Pentagon?

The Pentagon's power comes from the grip of an illusion, our own egos. The force of truth and love lived in their depths is a force of unity, of life itself. That force is real. We need to join in a community committed to that nonviolent life-force which is the power of the powerless. We need to test the truth by betting our lives on it in the world. If a community can experiment deeply enough in a nonviolent life-force, the power of the Pentagon will crumble.

I find that hard to believe.

So do I, but let's give it a try.

From the court record of United States of America, Plaintiff, **vs.** Kevin C. Patz, *et al.*, Defendants; Seattle, Washington; September 12, 1977 (one of many such trials of people who went onto the Trident submarine base to stop nuclear war).

The Clerk: State your full name and spell your last name for the record, please.

The Witness: Taeko Miwa, M-i-w-a.

By Ms. Lunam (another defendant, acting as her own attorney):

Q   Taeko, will you tell the Court where you live?

A   I live in Vancouver, B.C., Canada.

Q   Would you tell us what your citizenship is?

A   I am a Japanese citizen.

Q   Would you tell us why, as a non-American resident, you felt compelled to protest the American Trident missile system   (by going over the base fence)?

A   I have two reasons

One is, I originally am from Japan, which is the only country having the experience of an atomic bomb attack, and the disaster caused by it. . .When I was in Japan, back in Japan last year, I was a member of a peace mission with a couple of other Greenpeace members from North America. We stayed at atomic bomb survivors' hospitals. One of the survivors told us to the tell the people in North America what really happened to them and how the atomic bomb affected the people. The lady told us to work hard to prevent this kind of thing from happening again.

So, after this experience I have been feeling very strongly the responsibility for working on this.

That is one reason.

The other reason is that I am expecting a baby very soon, about three weeks from now. When I was doing   the actions on July 4th, I felt very strong and confident   about what I was doing. It was as if the baby in me was   telling me to do that or even at least the baby was demanding   all of us to prepare a very safe peaceful place for the baby,   and I was feeling all the mothers-to-be and fathers-to-be   throughout the world also hoping for a peaceful harmonious place   for future generations.

We chose the Trident campaign as our experiment in nonviolence in an end-time: standing firm to the end in hope of seeing a new world begin.

Trident is the leading edge of the nuclear arms race, "the ultimate first-strike weapon," as Trident's former missile-designer, Bob Aldridge, calls it. A Trident submarine will be 560 feet long (almost two football fields extended end to end) and will weigh 18,700 tons, even heavier than our newest nuclear strike cruisers. A single Trident sub will carry 24 missiles, each having as many as 17 independently targetted warheads. Thus a Trident sub will be able to destroy up to 408 cities or missile emplacements, each with a nuclear blast five times that which obliterated Hiroshima. Guidance systems will direct each of Trident's 408 warheads 6,000 miles so as to hit their targets within a few feet. This precision and power will give Trident, together with other U.S. counterforce weapons, the ability to launch a disarming first strike, destroying Soviet missiles in their silos and submarines and spewing enormous radioactivity over the world. [1]

As Bob Aldridge sums up Trident:

> The Trident II missile in the Trident submarine will be the ultimate counterforce system. In conjunction with a profound system of computer-integrated anti-submarine warfare weapons and sensors, Trident will give the United States first-strike capability. That is why I say Trident is the most lethal weapon ever built. [2]

We thought ourselves personally responsible for Trident because of its location, based at Bangor, Washington, 50 miles south of the Canadian border, near Seattle, with its missiles being designed and built by Lockheed in the San Francisco Bay Area. Trident is dependent on the acceptance, silence, and complicity of the many people in our Pacific area. We live next to the nuclear final solution, the ultimate first-strike weapon. Our American and Canadian governments are complicit in a nuclear first-strike policy. But in terms of building nonviolent resistance, Trident's route to the Pacific Ocean through the Canadian-American Strait of Juan de Fuca is ideal for the kind of transnational movement needed to stop nuclear war.

The choice of Trident for a nonviolent campaign was made also on grounds of faith and hope. The planning and development of Trident was far enough along, its priority so high in the Pentagon, that if Trident could be stopped by a grass roots movement emphasizing nonviolent direct action, then one could believe any destructive force could be turned around—even the nuclear age itself. In the context of our nuclear end-time, the Trident campaign in its nonviolent process, transnational character, and "impossible" goal, is a communal experiment in faith and hope which can help open up a new world or confirm the inevitability of our old one's destroying itself.

As a theologian of liberation says, "Faith is believing that there is hope for our world." [3] Despair is denying that our nuclear war systems can be stopped or changed. Faith is a commitment to the world's transformation through God to a kingdom of justice and peace. Faith's denial is mindlessness and hopelessness—yours and mine—in the face of the Pentagon and its corporations, a despair whose consequences for the world would have no parallel in history. Never before has our despair at changing institutions threatened the extinction of all life on earth. Faith is belief in a Reality, and a transformation, through which it is possible for us to live deeply enough to choose new life rather than nuclear death. A lived faith will stop the Bomb.

The decision to act on faith is always at hand. We live alongside the steady preparation for nuclear holocaust, as unseeing as were the onlookers of Nazi genocide. Yet the decision to act on faith is more possible for us in a liberal capitalism than it was for those who lived in fear alongside barbed-wire fences and guard towers in Europe in the 40's, and who because they didn't act, gave up hope for the rest of their world. Despair at political change comes from the heart. Given hearts rooted in faith, barbed-wire fences can themselves become openings to the belief that there is hope for our world.

On our first trip over the Trident base fence, July 4, 1975, 30 of us planted a vegetable garden on the base, to say that the Trident system's $60 billion could be better used in feeding people. At that time we had little understanding of the base security system. But we did know that it was already a high-security base with Polaris/Poseidon nuclear warheads stored on it. In our nonviolence training for the civil disobedience, we had role-played being shot at and attacked by police dogs—real anticipations that hot Fourth of July afternoon as we clambered over the barbed-wire fence with our shovels, hoes, and seedlings.

Minutes after our garden was planted, we were surrounded by security trucks. A guard demanded through a loudspeaker that we climb back over the fence or face arrest. We caucused, then sent our spokespersons forward to communicate our refusal to go back. A second demand was made, that we get into the security trucks. We refused again. Finally the guards negotiated with us. Our position, now that our garden had been planted, was that our further purpose that day was to walk the mile inside the fence to the main gate sowing wheat along the way. Then we would leave. After radioed consultations, the Navy agreed to our plan on condition that no more of our 125 supporters come over the fence. (No one in the support group had in fact planned on coming in.) So our first day of civil disobedience at the Trident base ended with a joyful celebration march and sowing of wheat on the base roads, escorted by security trucks, and with our friends just outside the fence singing and dancing along with us. We were released without charge. It had been a first act of faith in response to the fence, an initial overcoming of fear.

We believe Trident can be stopped if we are willing to experiment in the truth of nonviolence and give our lives for it.

Trident can be stopped if we can speak the truth over and over again that workers on the Trident base are good people whom we respect and that the weapons system they and we are complicit in building is the Auschwitz of Puget Sound. The truth which has to be realized consists of both of these: good people and the inconceivable evil of Trident—an evil which can then be stopped.

Trident can be stopped if we can realize that all of us, on both sides of the fence and the world, are one in God's love, in the humanity we share and are on the verge of annihilating. We can realize our unity in a process of truth and love which Jesus called "the kingdom of God" and Gandhi called "satyagraha" or "truth-force." The Trident campaign is an experiment in the truth-force of God's kingdom here and now, in our midst—a force of truth and love more powerful than the hydrogen bomb.

Trident can be stopped because good is more powerful than evil. But we have to believe in the good and live it out. Then anything can happen, beginning with the end of Trident.

In a sense beyond sense, the purpose of the Trident campaign is not to stop the Trident submarine and missile system. Its purpose is to change ourselves—all of us—so that there will no longer be anyone to run the submarine or fire the missile. At that point Trident will be stopped, but not as a primary goal and not by any opposing force. Trident will be stopped because the spirit in which we all live will have changed to the point of reducing Trident to what it is in truth: An inert holocaust machine which conscientious people will no more choose to operate than they would an Auschwitz oven. When we become different in truth and in the Spirit, there will simply be no one to run Trident.

In terms of an underlying reality, the goal of the Trident campaign is therefore not a political victory but spiritual change, a direct consequence of which would be the effective end of a system of death which no one can justify (and which everyone would then cease operating and trying to justify). This is the process of spiritual change which Gandhi called "satyagraha," a word which combines the Hindi terms for truth (*satya*) and force (*agraha*).

Anima Bose, a respected scholar of Gandhian nonviolence teaching at a university in India, has observed that the Trident campaign is one of the few contemporary experiments in a satyagraha campaign as defined by Gandhi.

Gandhi said of satyagraha:

> Its root meaning is holding on to truth, hence Truth-force. I have also called it Love-force or Soul-force. In the application of Satyagraha I discovered in the earliest stages that pursuit of truth did not admit of violence being inflicted on one's opponents but that they must be weaned from error by patience and sympathy. For what appears to be truth to the one may appear to be error to the other. And patience means self-suffering. So the doctrine came to mean vindication of Truth not by infliction of suffering on the opponent but on one's self.[4]

Satyagraha is truth-force, love-force, soul-force—words describing a process of spiritual transformation which goes far beyond the usual meanings attached to "nonviolence." Satyagraha is rooted in the belief that truth/love/soul-force is the most powerful force in existence, a spiritual reality as unexplored today as the power of the atom was a century ago. The other side of truth is love, and the union of the two in our hearts and lives is the overwhelming presence of God. As satyagraha, the Trident campaign is an experiment in uniting truth and love, personally and socially, so that we can begin to realize the presence of God in our midst and thus reject the terrible choice of destroying humankind by nuclear war.

Gandhi went on to say that satyagraha is "a process of educating public opinion, such that it covers all the elements of society and in the end makes itself irresistible. Violence interrupts the process and prolongs the real revolution of the whole social structure."

"The conditions necessary for the success of Satyagraha are: 1) The Satyagrahis should not have any hatred in their hearts against the opponent. 2) The issue must be true and substantial. 3) The Satyagrahis must be prepared to suffer till the end for the cause."[5]

Before applying these conditions to the Trident campaign, we should briefly summarize what has happened. Since the campaign began in 1975, more than a thousand people have engaged in civil disobedience. Many times that number have attended rallies, marched, kept vigil, and passed out leaflets at Bangor. In December 1977, in order to maintain a continuous nonviolent presence at Bangor, Ground Zero Center for Nonviolent Action was established alongside the fence of the base. Ground Zero's weekly leafleting of the Trident base, with positive challenging messages, has been—together with civil disobedience—the mainstay of our satyagraha campaign. The love-truth dynamic of the Trident campaign is evident in the two actions of leafleting and civil disobedience, a dynamic of dialogue and resistance.

The Satyagrahis should not have any hatred in their hearts against the opponent.

For 220 consecutive weeks in the campaign, Ground Zero people have passed out a new leaflet each week to workers driving into each of the gates at Naval Submarine Base Bangor, and more recently, to workers entering other Trident-related military sites. We have also passed out buttons saying "I'd rather make toys," and on each Thanksgiving, hundreds of freshly baked loaves of bread. Our first purpose in leafleting has been one of demonstrating our intention and attitude: to respect and will the good of each worker driving past us whether or not he or she accepts a leaflet—to hold that person within as a brother or sister, a primary attitude of nonviolence.

A second purpose in leafleting has been to seek a common truth in our leaflets—not to assert a protest against base workers but to discover a truth deep enough to be shared from either side of the Bangor fence. In writing leaflets which seek this common bond we have felt that humor is often more to the point than righteousness, and openness to dialogue more helpful than lectures. We have tried to speak a challenging truth about Trident and the arms race but not against those on the other side of the fence, who belong to the same family we do and will always have parts of the truth unseen by us.

A more personal dialogue than leafleting takes place in the homes of workers and Navy personnel living in Kitsap County, the extremely conservative rural area where the Bangor base is located. Our family's decision to move down from British Columbia and live in Kitsap County while working out of Ground Zero has made us neighbors and friends of people who have never known personally a "protester." Kitsap house meetings are held at which the Trident campaign is shared with such friends, who would be afraid to be seen publicly at an anti-Trident gathering.

In 1981–82 four key Bangor workers resigned their jobs for reasons of conscience and gave strong public support to the Trident campaign. All had been affected by the nonviolent dynamic of dialogue and resistance, love and truth. We believe the lives of these friends are deep signs of hope for the future.

The issue must be true and substantial.

The issue of the Trident campaign is life itself. Life is sacred. Deploying a first-strike nuclear weapons system which threatens all life on earth is a sin and a crime beyond all reckoning. We are concerned with the truest, most substantial issue of history—the preservation of life itself, through nonviolent faith and action. As we hear increasingly of resignations and noncooperation within the base for moral reasons, we sense a deepening recognition of that issue. All kinds of fences are beginning to come down.

The Satyagrahis must be prepared to suffer till the end for the cause.

Besides dialogue toward a deeper, more inclusive truth, a satyagraha or "truth-force" campaign also involves active resistance to this threat to life itself. On the resistance side of the campaign, civil disobedience to Trident has included a series of small-group actions which have gradually increased to mass actions involving hundreds of people climbing the base fence and going to jail. The largest civil disobedience was on May 22–23, 1978, as the first U.N. Special Session on Disarmament began, when 4,000 people marched to the base and 300 were arrested for climbing over the fence and displaying an enormous United Nations flag on the side of a hill. After the planting of our 1975 vegetable garden, small-group acts of resistance have included people going into the base to dig graves, giving out candy canes to kids living on the base (with the resisters dressing as clowns), praying at nuclear weapons bunkers, having a picnic, and talking with workers at different base facilities. In one major action Bangor's fence was cut down so that the "Trident Monster," a 560-foot-long portable symbol of Trident, could be marched onto the base. Other Bangor entries have included landing boats on its Hood Canal beach and swimming into the base.

Repeaters in civil disobedience have served escalating sentences of up to six months per conviction. The acceptance of fairly heavy jail sentences is in order to take on personal responsibility and suffering for Trident and to appeal to others for a deep change of heart.

The change of heart sought in the Trident campaign begins by each of us resolving to live out the truth as he or she sees it: Ground Zero people have to climb fences and block submarines to say with our lives that we are all on the edge of spiritual change or total destruction. We have to be prepared to risk our lives and go to jail for the sake of the truth as we see it. There is too much at stake—life itself—for us to do less.

At the same time, if questioning nuclear weapons converts Trident workers to a new truth, God will give them the power to resign their jobs and will sustain them and their families in other ways: Seek first the kingdom of God, and everything you need will be provided. That truth of Providence as taught by Jesus in the Sermon on the Mount is more firmly rooted in reality than any physical law. If followed, it is a truth that provides a security one can find nowhere else on earth, least of all through nuclear weapons.

An example of this is found in the lives of Al and Jerrie Drinkwine.

On August 12, 1982, the day on which the first Trident submarine, the USS Ohio, arrived at its Bangor base, Al Drinkwine resigned his $22,000 a year job inside the base. Al and Jerrie Drinkwine's decision that their family not be sustained by what they call the "immoral nuclear buildup" came after long reflection.

Al had been reading leaflets passed out to Bangor workers by Ground Zero volunteers every Thursday morning since September 1978. In the Winter of 1982 Al and Jerrie attended a meeting at Ground Zero, at the invitation of their friend, Father David Becker, who was in the process of resigning his position as Bangor Catholic Chaplain because of his moral opposition to Trident.

In June 1982 Al Drinkwine risked his job by testifying in a Kitsap County court in support of an arrested Ground Zero leafleter. Al stated his belief that Ground Zero had a right to leaflet and that the weekly leaflets gave Bangor workers hope that "there was another way."

The arrival of the USS Ohio prompted Al and Jerrie to choose another way. A month later they wrote the following letter to Bangor friends and workers, which was then passed out as a Ground Zero leaflet to workers entering the base.

September, 1982

Dear Friends and Neighbors,

When my wife and I were asked if we would write a letter for use in leafleting, which would address the reason I left my position at Bangor, our first reaction was, "Lord, why us? Don't you know how painful the decision to leave was! I'd like to leave quietly, but you say you need more."

Firstly, we consider ourselves the average, all-American family. We are one couple, three children, one niece, a dog and two cats, living happily under one roof. After high school, I served with the Air Force for four years, which enabled me to gain my B.A. through the G.I. Bill. Our first home was purchased through a VA loan. The day I was selected for my position with the Navy was a day we all celebrated. The government has been good to us. We are more than grateful.

During the past 7 years, we couldn't help but become more aware of the American economy, the mission of Bangor, and how they directly interacted. This developed into many inner conflicts: Social service and educational programs are being stripped to the bone. We've witnessed hunger in our own community. While on the other hand, extravagance flourishes at Bangor. . . . We felt the comfort of job security, but could no longer ignore the anguish it contributed to others around us.

Ultimately, the greatest questions of all still loomed over us. As a person, a couple, a family in the human race, do we honestly believe that "peace at any price" is how our Creator wishes us to live? Peace, at the expense of all humankind? Is it right to use nuclear arms against any other human in the name of defense, or peace? Could we continue being instruments in the potential destruction of all life?

This year's Armed Forces Day theme of "Peace Through Strength" blatantly portrayed an attitude being passed down to our children. As we walked through the hallway of our elementary school, we observed pictures the students drew depicting this theme. The majority were drawings of bombings, killings, machine guns, warships and warfare. What kind of hope does this attitude offer the next generation? It is our firm belief that our strength does not come from military power, built out of fear; but rather, it is a gift from God which we have the responsibility to nourish and give thanks for.

We *are* a great nation! As world leaders, it is our task, and privilege, to reach out and show others alternatives to warfare. Suicide has always been the easy way out. At best, that's the only promise a nuclear war offers. We, as people, are being called and challenged to use our talents, skills and gifts in a more life-giving manner. We believe in America. We can meet that challenge by working together and creating those alternatives.

Lovingly,
Al and Jerrie Drinkwine

The nonviolent process of the Trident campaign has touched people beyond the Bangor base, including Seattle Catholic Archbishop Raymond Hunthausen.

In the fall of 1976 Archbishop Hunthausen asked all the priests in the Seattle archdiocese to consider joining in prayer and fasting in support of a 30-day fast by members of the Trident campaign, who were appealing to the presidential candidates to renounce the first use of nuclear weapons. The following spring Archbishop Hunthausen sent his clergy a resource booklet with the title, "Repent Trident," suggesting that they preach on this theme. In 1979 the Archbishop attended his first Bangor demonstration. In 1981 he identified Trident as "the Auschwitz of Puget Sound" and spoke in favor of unilateral disarmament as an expression of the cross of Christ. His subsequent tax resistance to nuclear weapons has been his personal statement for unilateral disarmament.

In August 1982 Archbishop Hunthausen and the other religious leaders of the Church Council of Greater Seattle kept vigil together in a sailboat in support of the Peace Blockade, which tried to stop the first Trident submarine with rowboats. Archbishop Hunthausen's prophetic voice and actions have profoundly deepened the spiritual center of the Trident campaign. He has helped to keep us focused on love as the center of nonviolence, truth as a mutual sharing across the fence, and conversion as a constant inner call to us all.

In a satyagraha campaign, unlike war, it is the force of truth and love which determines the outcome—not violence and not even political pressures. The purpose of the Trident campaign is to awaken that nonviolent, love-truth force in everyone, on both sides of the fence. We all need conversion to a new spirit of nonviolence. Through such an ongoing conversion Trident can be stopped.

Beneath the nonviolent dynamic of dialogue and resistance, then, is the conversion of the heart. The process of opening our hearts to conversion means accepting suffering out of love. Nonviolent resistance to the Trident submarine is an outward expression of our ongoing conversion from the Tridents within, carried out in suffering love. Thus suffering violence out of love for the other, while speaking and acting out the truth, is the nonviolent way not simply to convert an opponent but to transform the very situation in which the opponent and we are living—a double conversion. That is the process we are discovering more deeply in the Trident campaign.

The double conversion we are seeking might become visible by widespread resignations of Trident jobs and by tens of thousands of people expressing their willingness to be jailed for loving disobedience to Trident. Or, because we ourselves are subjects of the conversion we seek, transformation of the situation may surface—in fact almost certainly will—in ways totally unforeseen by Ground Zero people. In any case, the way to such nonviolent change, as discovered by Jesus and Gandhi, is through suffering love in "experiments in truth"; absorbing violence out of love for the sake of the emerging truth we both bear witness to and seek in deeper forms.

Our Peace Blockade of the USS Ohio in August 1982 offers a way to reflect critically on the process of the Trident campaign, in terms of a resistance action which took place seven years after the campaign's beginning. Was the August 12, 1982 Peace Blockade of the first Trident submarine, the USS Ohio, a truly nonviolent action?

The "Battle of Oak Bay," as the news media called it (a "battle" in which only one side had weapons), pitted a Coast Guard fleet of 99 ships against our two flagships, two launches, a canoe, and 16 row-boats. The Coast Guard used water hoses extensively, and threatened the use of machine guns, M-16 rifles, and pistols. The government used the Coast Guard to launch a first strike on the Peace Blockade, making preemptive arrests at dawn on August 12 before the Ohio was in sight. It then dropped its charges one week later.

According to the media, the Coast Guard won. They prevented all but two Blockade boats from approaching the Ohio, and the Ohio did not stop. (In fact the Ohio had stopped earlier, several miles to the north, awaiting word that the preemptive arrests had removed block-aders.) The scene was volatile, the use of the heavier weapons being threatened by nervous hands and heads. One reporter has written that had a firecracker gone off at a critical moment, a massacre could have resulted.

The Coast Guard's preparation for a possible massacre was, I think, the result of a higher order to "clear the protesters out of the way of the Ohio by any means necessary"—leaving the details of that, as at My Lai, to subordinate officers. Those surprised by the threatened use of such force should not have been. It was being deployed to protect history's most destructive weapons system from what the government perceived as the humiliation of being confronted and possibly stopped by "a ragtag fleet," an example it wished to discourage.

The immediate question of nonviolence on August 12 was, in Gandhian, Christian terms, one of response to violence: Did we suffer the violence in love?

A scene I witnessed on our Peace Blockade trimaran, the Lizard of Woz, was that of Eve and Ted Phillips saying repeatedly to a Coast Guard officer, holding a pistol to Ted's back, that they loved him. I joined them in that, and we said the Lord's Prayer together while kneeling by the officer. Did we love our Coast Guard brother deeply enough? Not enough to disarm him; perhaps enough to prevent a shooting. The pistol in Ted's back was cocked, and the finger on its trigger shaking.

Had the trigger been pulled, I believe Eve would even then have loved the Coast Guard officer. Her nonviolence, from a Christ-centered faith and love, is radiant and profound. In reflecting back on that moment, I believe it may have saved Ted's life.

How strong our blockading community as a whole would have been in our love of someone responsible for a shooting I don't know. As things turned out, I believe we were too concerned after the blockade with the Coast Guard's treatment of us. The handling we experienced was not gentle. It was consistent with the policies Trident was made to protect. The same government has been to Vietnam and El Salvador. By resisting Trident with out whole lives in the Peace Blockade we had the momentary experience of being treated in return like peasants under imperialism. The guns were trained on us. Yet nonviolence is a steadfast love, in resistance, of the people behind those guns, no matter what they do. It is that force of unrelenting love which can overcome anything.

It is often claimed that Trident is protecting the protesters' freedom to protest. In fact, it is protecting the privileges of American power, shared by Peace Blockaders to the extent that we accept the assumptions of our being somehow different and privileged. In our insistence on our rights after arrest I felt a tone of indignation that we were being treated like other people in the world. Our only real power in nonviolence is to stand with those people (or lie bound with them), and to continue to love more deeply.

The Peace Blockade was always incapable of "winning the Battle of Oak Bay," if the government were to choose—as it did—to deploy the force at its command. But nonviolence was never meant to win battles. It is meant to turn the battles into new directions, for everyone concerned.

The Peace Blockade raised for some the question of our provoking violence. A "Peace Blockade" was said to be a contradiction in terms. It was said to be too confrontational, too military in nature, to be nonviolent—a point made especially by editorial writers and military commanders. The military people seemed to believe, as the encounter with the Ohio neared, that between the Peace Blockade and the U.S. Navy there was "a rowboat gap"—an acknowledgment that Ernie Baird (Peace Blockade Boat Building Director) makes a more sturdy boat than General Dynamics does.

The sobering truth in those rowboat-gap statements was the underlying sense of threat felt by speakers on behalf of the militarism which now controls the United States government. It was a glimpse into just how rarely in the peace movement we choose actions which are confrontational enough to state the seriousness of nonviolence, and a glimpse into the power of such actions over the most destructive, therefore most empty, military force in history. The government knew it had to keep our rowboats away from the Ohio. Our rowboats were a force more powerful than Trident. People who love life to the point of risking their lives for peace express a spiritual force whose ultimate power is unknown.

I was startled by the power of nonviolence in the days before the Ohio's arrival when the government kept parading its Coast Guard armada, in D-Day-type formations, past our Peace Blockade mother-duckling maneuvers. Not only was the government shutting down 18 miles of the Hood Canal in an unprecedented security measure, but it had called out a fleet larger than some nations' navies to corral our blockade flotilla. It made one wonder. Choosing nonviolence in the right place—directly in front of a holocaust machine—could make a difference. At least our military friends realized that. Maybe we should, too, and make more choices of that kind.

The Peace Blockade was just confrontational enough to give one a sense of nonviolent revolution, really changing our lives and our structures, as distinct from crying out in the night.

While the Peace Blockade was incapable of winning any military battles, it succeeded in deeper ways. Ground Zero member Karol Schulkin has recounted some of them:

> There was the response of the Coast Guard man who was aiming his water hose at 78-year-old Peace Blockader Ruth Youngdahl Nelson. She looked up at him and said, "Young man, not in my America, please." He laid down his hose and walked away.
>
> There was the woman who drove her van into the base camp with the "Welcome USS Ohio" banner on the side. She didn't agree with us she said, but she was a Christian. She knew the campground had

no water supply. For days afterwards she brought us large cans of water, and loaves of bread as well.

There was the federal marshal who spent hours accompanying the prisoners from the Bangor base to the Federal Court House in Seattle. As the journey ended he asked a woman prisoner, with whom he had been dialoguing, for her peace button. He pinned it on his uniform above his badge.

There was the Coast Guard man who drove to Ground Zero to apologize for the harsh treatment people had received and who stayed to talk for several hours with a volunteer who had served in the Coast Guard himself some years before.

There was the crew member of the USS Ohio who came the next day to talk with us at the court-house steps. He told how he and a number of the crew agreed with us—that Trident was a dangerous weapon and needed to be stopped.

And there was the Trident base worker, husband and father of three, who resigned his job in protest the day the Ohio arrived; and another worker who knelt in prayer at the dockside ceremony while others cheered and the band played "Anchors Aweigh."[6]

The power for change in the Peace Blockade was a largely invisible one even to those expressing it. We identified too much with the action of blockading, some of us feeling afterwards that we had to blockade again, as soon as possible, if we were to stop Trident. The loving, nonviolent process of stopping Trident was expressed through the blockade, at the same time as it went deeper than that action. We found it hard to leave it behind, when the spirit had been expressed through it.

Blockading was the action, but the power for change was the spirit of love running through it. Love has to find ways to meet the holocaust head on, and break open the personal/collective power of our souls. We experienced the blockade as a beginning way for love to meet death and explode into the soul-force Gandhi felt and the resurrection Jesus promised.

The power for change in the Peace Blockade wasn't just in blockading the Ohio. The inner power for change was in a love that was willing to suffer. Had we blockaded the Ohio in any other spirit, we would have lost everything.

Was the Peace Blockade nonviolent?

As measured by Jesus' and Gandhi's criterion of suffering love for the sake of truth, I believe it was nonviolent—sometimes profoundly so and sometimes by a hairline only. Conversion and transformation remain down the road, (or down the Hood Canal) from the blockade. We would have to learn a deeper, more disciplined, more loving process for future nonviolent action, a process that can be sustained and intensified to the point of transformation.

There is a mystery of love involved in the Trident campaign. This was present in the Peace Blockade. But it has come home to us especially in recent years in the form of the Peace Pagoda. The coming of the Peace Pagoda to Ground Zero is an event which has given further meaning to lightning striking from east to west.

In the spring of 1979 Suzuki, a Japanese Buddhist monk, came to Ground Zero because he was attracted by its spirit of nonviolence. Suzuki arrived at our doorstep and discovered that a Buddha had been sent to him in the mail, and this he took as a confirming sign of his calling to Ground Zero. He stayed with us three years.

In the first year Suzuki followed his spiritual discipline by walking around the Trident base, chanting outside its fence, "NaMuMyoHo-RengeKo." He also shared with us his vision that the first Peace Pagoda in the United States would be built at Ground Zero, alongside the fence of the most destructive site in Western civilization. Suzuki's Nipponzan Myohoji Order had built over 50 Peace Pagodas, usually in sacred places in the Far East. The purpose of the pagodas is to fulfill the Lord Buddha's teaching in the Lotus Sutra; "When it seems all are burning, my land will be safe." Constructing Peace Pagodas will realize a widening peace at a time that threatens universal fire.

During his second year at Ground Zero, Suzuki brought into our midst his venerable 97-year-old master, Nichidatsu Fujii. We were won over by the love and wisdom of "Gurudji," who came to visit Ground Zero on the night Ronald Reagan was elected President of the United States. That night was a time of spiritual revival at Ground Zero, expressed in three religious traditions: the Nichiren Buddhism of Gurudji and his chanting monks and nuns; the Native American tradition of Tullalip elder Janet McCloud; the Christian faith of our Ground Zero prayer group. Whatever Reagan's presidency might bring, that night promised a time of deepening spiritual power at Ground Zero.

On the following day when Gurudji was shown around Ground Zero, he decided that the first Peace Pagoda in the United States should be built there. The pagoda would radiate peace to the base, as Ground Zero had sought to do in other ways. Gurudji said that his experience while living in Gandhi's ashram in India was his reason for believing that Ground Zero was a sacred place. Just as people went willingly to jail from Gandhi's ashram, so, too, did people from Ground Zero make that sacrifice. And that made the Ground Zero land sacred—a proper site for the Peace Pagoda.

In Suzuki's third year at Ground Zero, he was joined by a growing community of monks who began construction of the Peace Pagoda. But as the power and symbolism of the pagoda became more widely known in the military context of Kitsap County, opposition to it built up. The project was halted abruptly by the Kitsap County commissioners, who refused to grant a bulding permit for it. They claimed that according to the zoning code Ground Zero was incompatible with our neighbors to the west, the Trident base.

Shortly after the commissioners' decision was made public, a geodesic dome at Ground Zero was burnt to the ground. The monks had been chanting in it every morning. The unidentified arsonists had poured a flammable substance around the temporary altar where the Buddha for the pagoda rested. But in burning the Buddha the arsonists also burnt Christ. Opposite the Buddha had been a crucifix. The symbols of compassion and love were fused by fire. The spirit of that vision moved us to issue a public statement asking forgiveness from the burners for any violence we might have caused them in provoking their attack.

Eight months later a judge overruled the Kitsap commissioners' decision: The Peace Pagoda could be built. By that time, Suzuki was no longer with us, having become a pilgrim to other places. We thank him in our hearts for the gift of peace to Ground Zero which has come through his life.

The mystery of the Peace Pagoda, the continuing mystery of the Trident campaign, is a mystery of Love. Love has brought our lives together in a mysterious way, and Love will sustain us in the truth-force we experience and become. Seek first the kingdom, and all these things shall be yours as well.

The hope of the Peace Blockade and the Peace Pagoda, the continuing hope of the Trident campaign, is to resist a doomsday machine in such a way as to realize a profound unity in the world—in and through the very act of resistance. To do that we must resist Trident not by some means external to ourselves, a form of violence, but by actions which deepen our own lives at the same time as they touch others.

The struggle of such a campaign is to resist a killing machine while always seeking our inner unity, one discovered in silence, and our unity with the people involved in the machine, who are never the same as the machine. Satyagraha, or truth-force, confronts the world of injustice in direct action while seeing the people of that world from within, as belonging to a vast unity of life. We struggle to confront death and discover our inner life at the same time. It is the inner side of the campaign which will be decisive in both overcoming Trident and realizing oneness in the world. We rediscover that oneness by going deeper than our own Tridents: inner assumptions of the ego, fears about reality which divide us from the unity of life.

The Trident campaign as an experiment in truth-force is meant to connect with the lives of all people, all threatened by nuclear death. If we were so graced as to feel the most distant life at its center, we would know from within its pain and compassion, its loneliness and its love— the human feelings of Jesus and of Hitler, as different as they were in acting those out and failing to do so. There is no one who doesn't feel at the deepest levels something of our living unity. An experiment in truth-force is meant to touch that level in everyone.

Trident with its thousands of Hiroshimas is the end of the world. The Trident campaign is meant to re-discover a new world, one world, the only world remaining. The campaign can be seen as both spirit and body: Seeking first the kingdom of a deepening, widening community . . . in and through experiments of nonviolent direct action. Renouncing any fixation on the fruits of action . . . while trying to choose actions which in themselves carry the seeds of a moral and political crisis. Discovering life . . . through a faith willing to suffer.

The Christian experience of faith is in a God of hope to humanity, a loving God who will finally bring justice and peace to the world. The Christian prays, "Thy kingdom come," knowing that when the kingdom does come, swords will be beaten into plowshares—or more difficult to believe today, that nuclear weapons will be abolished and the world's masses freed from hunger and oppression. The Christian experience of faith is in a God who will finally transform the world as we know it, filled with violence and suffering, into a new heaven and new earth where love and truth will reign in people's hearts and be embodied in a global community. Thus faith in God means hope for the earth, a hope for all of humanity.

Christians hold in common this hope toward an ultimate justice and peace for the world, "the kingdom of God." They differ about whether this new earth will be in or out of time, and they differ on the extent to which they are themselves responsible for bringing it about.

The most popular Christian view of a new earth is that it will occur at the very end of time or somewhere beyond time, and that God alone will bring it about—with only one human instrument, the returning Christ. This view of a "Vertical Coming" of the new earth sees God, as it were from above, striking an abrupt end to history. Only through Christ's Second Coming, and with no other human mediation, will the old earth suddenly give way—at the end of time and beyond it—to the new. What faithful humans can do in the meantime is simply watch and wait, as the Gospels tell us. The Vertical Coming is found in the New Testament, though not in the form it has taken in our own time. It was originally preached by poor apostles as a vision of hope to the poor and suffering, who could expect a final justice. Today the Vertical Coming of the new earth has lost favor with the poor because they have heard so much of it from the rich, who profit while the poor watch and wait for a justice beyond time.

A second Christian view of the kingdom, or the new earth, is that it will occur somewhere within time, as a culmination of human struggle through the power of God. If one were to eliminate that final phrase, "through the power of God," this second view is similar to the Marxist vision of history—a vision of people struggling toward a new earth, a society of justice where it will be from each according to her ability, to each according to her need. The kingdom of God on earth is its description for Christians. Or one could call it the Horizontal Coming, the coming of the kingdom from within history. And it, too, has sources in the New Testament: "Thy kingdom come, thy will be done, on earth as it is in heaven." Or the parables of Jesus where the kingdom is seen as a leaven, a seed, or a tree, in a process of growth rather than coming only through the intervention of a God beyond history. The Horizontal Coming of the new earth is a process whereby God is already present in history, and becomes embodied in the struggles of the poor for their liberation.

The first point to note about the two Christian views of the kingdom's coming, the Vertical and the Horizontal, is that both views agree in seeing total justice and peace as the goal of history. However perverted it has become in a capitalist society, the Christian faith by everyone's definition is faith in a God of ultimate and complete justice. Whoever experiences this faith experiences the hope that we will finally live in justice and peace.

Perhaps the view of Jesus himself lay somewhere in a combination of the Vertical and Horizontal Comings of the kingdom. The original feature of Albert Schweitzer's interpretation of Jesus, and of the kingdom of God, is that Jesus tried to "force"—that is, he tried to activate or precipitate—the coming of the kingdom. Schweitzer thought that Jesus, by the movement of metanoia and then by his suffering and death, sought to fulfill humanly the divine conditions of the sudden breaking in of the kingdom. A special value of Schweitzer's apocalyptic-activist view of Jesus is that it opens up the way in which the human being, Jesus, experimented toward a transforming truth in what he saw as an end-time. In Gandhi's terms, Jesus was experimenting more and more deeply in truth—in an age and place where truth took the form of apocalyptic revolutions, when it was felt that the deepest human experience of truth could prepare the coming of the kingdom of God on earth.

Thus the question is raised: What did Jesus discover? Not: What did Jesus, the Son of God, reveal? Rather: What did Jesus, the human being, discover—in his experiments toward a transforming truth, and in what he perceived as an end-time? What in the depths of Jesus' life gave birth to the transforming power of the Gospels, as these have been transmitted to us?

The question is not one which can be answered in a definitive way. But it can be explored in such a way as to open up the question of our own end-time's transformation. Jesus was seeking such a transformation. And if we can look on him as a brother, opening up a way, we may be helped by him in seeing the beginning of a transforming way for ourselves.

In his *Asian Journal*, Thomas Merton describes a transforming way which opened up for him, the experience given to him in his contemplation of the great stone Buddhas at Polonnaruwa in Ceylon one week before he died:

> I am able to approach the Buddhas barefoot and undisturbed, my feet in wet grass, wet sand. Then the silence of the extraordinary faces. The great smiles. Huge and yet subtle. Filled with every possibility, questioning nothing, knowing everything, rejecting nothing, the peace not of emotional resignation but of Madhyamika, of sunyata, that has seen through every question without trying to discredit anyone or anything—*without refutation*—

without establishing some other argument. For the doctrinaire, the mind that needs well-established positions, such peace, such silence, can be frightening. . .

Looking at these figures I was suddenly, almost forcibly, jerked clean out of the habitual, half-tied vision of things, and an inner clearness, clarity, as if exploding from the rocks themselves, became evident and obvious. . .The thing about all this is that there is no puzzle, no problem, and really no "mystery." All problems are resolved and everything is clear, simply because what matters is clear. The rock, all matter, all life is charged with dharmakaya . . . everything is emptiness and everything is compassion.[7]

Everything is emptiness and everything is compassion. In our resistance to humankind's destruction, we need to live and act in that spirit of ultimate perfect emptiness and compassion if we are to experience a way of transformation.

Along such a way, there is no us and them, no problem of evil fixed insolubly in the lives of others. The truth is that there is no intentional evil or sin of which we can be certain except our own. It is thus our own sin which is the metaphysical key to the apparent sin of all—an insight with shattering political implications which is the undiscovered basis of Gandhi's vision of nonviolence identifying profound personal change with a global transformation. One can make an analogy to Einstein's scientifically revolutionary formulation: Just as mass is resistance to change but in the process of change (i.e., motion) has energy, so is sin resistance to change but which nevertheless can be converted into great energy for change. If I can know for certain in reality only the responsibility of my own sin, then the essence of reality involves my accepting as an extension of that insight the responsibility for all evil—turning a recognition of the radical nature and extension of sin into a new energy for revolutionary personal/social change. Our own sin can, through a responsible insight, be converted into an undiscovered energy for change. We are all one, and the person responsible for global evils, as confirmed by our own radical insight into consciousness, is not somewhere out there but right here.

But as Gandhi taught—together with Dostoevsky in *The Brothers Karamazov*, and basic to them both, Jesus in the Gospels—because an experiment in this reality has to go so deeply into ego-shattering truths, we seldom experience the primary truth: the responsibility of each for all through the recognition of one's own sin as fundamental to the most destructive violence and evil, as seen in widening circles from one's own immediate situation (the first sin-barrier we refuse to acknowledge and cross) extending outward to the entire world. Without denying that evil has many external agents in the world, its ultimate source and responsibility comes home with startling clarity when we are finally humbled enough by reality to see simply and clearly—that as we are, so is the world. At that point, we become open to Merton's way of transformation, as experienced in his encounter with the Buddhas, where everything is emptiness and everything is compassion. We begin then to walk on that transforming way of ultimate perfect emptiness and compassion.

In our valley in the mountains of British Columbia where I am writing this, the native people once went on vision-quests into the Reality of the valley. There are still ancient reminders of those vision-quests, to be discovered today by the lonely person of vision who continues to walk the valley floor and to explore its rock walls in pursuit of an ancient and present truth. There is one such person who is our friend, and because of him, David Kurkhonen, we have been led to see the pictographs, symbolic paintings done by the Indians on boulders at the foot of great cliffs and rock slides. These pictographs of trees, animals, persons, and unexplained visions sketched by a people on our valley rocks hundreds of years ago are our invitation into a unified Reality, a Oneness of Being, lost with the passing of that people. The pictographs are an invitation into Reality, like the wind passing through the pine trees all around them.

At the bottom of one rock slide in our valley, there is another expression of a vision-quest, a low, rock wall with strange outcroppings moving aimlessly (aimlessly in terms of walls which act as barriers) along the foot of the slide for several hundred feet, obscured by trees and boulders. A wall—or more accurately, a rock sculpture—whose meandering form was built up patiently by a person who once saw a vision, perhaps while on retreat on the cliffs high above, which demanded form in the world. The vision of that strange sculpture was formed out of piled rocks, for months and maybe years on end, so that the person, or community of persons, who had sensed it could live in truth and peace.

In our nuclear end-time, a vision of the kingdom demands concrete expression in the world if we are to live in truth and peace.

We need the patience and single-mindedness to form that vision of a global community out of the rocks of our own lives and communities, and to build up a vision of the kingdom of God on earth, from life to life, from community to community. In our own valley of division and darkness, there is an invitation into Oneness, a transforming way to follow.

I believe that you and I are invited. We are invited over the fences into the heart of the Trident base. We are invited down through tunnels and through vaulted doors into the War Room of the Pentagon. We are invited into acts of ultimate perfect emptiness and compassion in the places of total destruction of life on earth. We are invited into these places because they are ours. In the nuclear age we live in darkness, in the absence of God, and the darkness is not separate from ourselves. Going to the heart of Bangor or the Pentagon will bring no revelation of destruction. We've been there every day of our lives. In a time of total violence, our love has grown cold.

In walking into the darkness of these places which we know already in ourselves, we may eventually discover a tiny ray of light. As we go more deeply with more faith and love into our own responsibility for darkness, that ray of light could intensify and fan out into the brilliance of a billion suns. The Light in our darkness is real. The transforming unity we seek is here.

1 Bob Aldridge has documented the first-strike technology of Trident in a series of articles for *The Nation*. The most definitive of these is "Trident—The Devil's Pitchfork," *The Nation* (December 27, 1980). The overall U.S. first-strike policy is evident in the current development of five major systems: 1) a space warfare ability to destroy the opponent's early warning and communications satellites; 2) extremely accurate missiles and bombers to destroy enemy missile silos and other land targets; 3) an antisubmarine warfare force able to sink hostile missile-launching submarines; 4) a ballistic missile and bomber defense capable of intercepting any surviving enemy missiles or aircraft that are launched in retaliation; and 5) an intricate network of command, control, and communication to coordinate and integrate 1 through 4. For the description of these interlocking systems see Robert C. Aldridge, *The Counterforce Syndrome* (pamphlet published in 1978 by the Institute for Policy Studies, 1901 Q Street, N.W., Washington, D.C. 20009).

Bob Aldridge's full-length study of U.S. nuclear policy, *First Strike*, will be published by South End Press in early 1983. This particular book will be as important for our understanding in the 1980's as Hitler's *Mein Kampf* was in the 1930's. Hopefully it will be more closely read. There is no single evil genius behind U.S. nuclear policy to write with open ambition its *Mein Kampf*. The anonymity and secrecy of U.S. policy is more sinister. At last someone, Bob Aldridge, has exposed this final evil with a clarity that will allow no excuse for not undertaking a nonviolent commitment to stop it.

2 Robert Aldridge, "By Land, Sea and Air," *Sojourners* (February 1977), p. 14.
3 Jose Miranda, *Marx and the Bible* (Orbis Books: 1974), p. 227.
4 M. K. Gandhi, *The Voice of Truth* (Navajivan Press: 1968), p. 179.
5 *Ibid.*, p. 186.
6 Karol Schulkin, "A Force More Powerful Than Trident," *Ground Zero* (October/November 1982), p. 11. The way to keep informed on the Trident campaign is to read *Ground Zero* 16159 Clear Creek Rd., N.W., Poulsbo, WA 98370.
7 *The Asian Journal of Thomas Merton* (New Directions: 1973), pp. 233-35.

FIND IT FAST